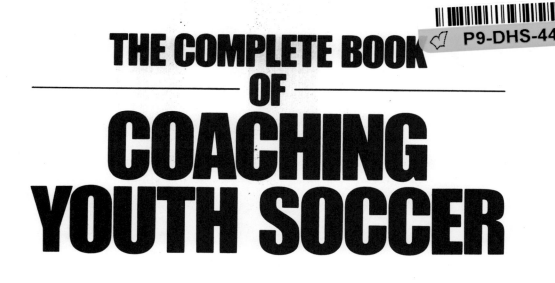

THE COMPLETE BOOK
OF
COACHING
YOUTH SOCCER

THE COMPLETE BOOK
OF
COACHING
YOUTH SOCCER

The Authoritative Guide to Successful Team Tactics and Competitive Individual Skills

Recommended by the

NYSCA
National Youth Sports Coaches Association

SIMON WHITEHEAD

CB
CONTEMPORARY BOOKS
A TRIBUNE NEW MEDIA/EDUCATION COMPANY

Library of Congress Cataloging-in-Publication Data

Whitehead, Simon.
    [Teaching of soccer]
    The complete book of coaching youth soccer / Simon Whitehead.
       p.   cm.
    Reprint. Originally published: The teaching of soccer. c1987.
    ISBN 0-8092-4072-6
    1. Soccer for children—United States—Coaching.   I. Title
GV943.8.W49   1991
796.334'07'7—dc20
                                        90-24285
                                            CIP

ACKNOWLEDGMENTS

For their assistance in the production of this book,
I would like to thank my editor, Jim Hoehn,
Robert L. Stoker, and Carrie Pickmosa.

Illustrations by Carrie Pickmosa
Diagrams by Simon Whitehead

Originally published as *The Teaching of Soccer: A Working
Manual for Youth Coaches* (Minneapolis: Educational
Sports Programs, Inc.), 1987.

Published by Contemporary Books, Inc.
Two Prudential Plaza, Chicago, Illinois 60601-6790
Manufactured in the United States of America
International Standard Book Number: 0-8092-4072-6

This book is dedicated to all those brave individuals,
whether parent or not, who have the courage to say,
"OK, I'll coach the team."

CONTENTS

Acknowledgments   *iv*
Legend for Figures   *viii*

Introduction   *1*
1   Aims, Objectives, and Teaching Hints   *4*
2   Organizational Tips   *8*
3   Juggling and Warm-Ups   *15*
4   Passing and Control   *22*
5   Ball Handling: Dribbling   *35*
6   Heading   *47*
7   Shooting and Volleying   *58*
8   Goalkeeping   *69*
9   Ball Winning and Defense   *82*
10   Throw-Ins, Goal Kicks, Corners, and Free Kicks   *89*
11   Game Drills and Positional Play   *98*
12   Team Formations   *114*
13   Summing Up   *120*

Appendix I: Basic Laws of Soccer   *122*
Appendix II: Successful Soccer   *123*
Appendix III: Ten-Week Season Plans   *128*
Glossary of Soccer Terms   *132*
Index   *134*

LEGEND FOR FIGURES

.... coach

.... attacking player

.... defending player

.... assisting player

.... ball in plan diagrams

.... ball in stick figure diagrams

.... cone or grid marker

.... path of player

.... path of ball

.... path of player moving with the ball

Note: **All units of measurement are in yards unless otherwise stated.**

INTRODUCTION

THE FIRST PRACTICE

The situation is all too familiar. It's the first session of your newly formed soccer team. Twenty beaming faces eagerly wait to be led by the intrepid new coach. The anxiety felt by "coach" on such an occasion is comparable to that felt when taking a driving test, going for a job interview, or giving a presentation before a large crowd.

After all, you probably took the job only because no one else would. Or maybe you thought, "I've got to be able to do better than the last fellow." You may have a youngster playing and are amazed at his or her ever-developing skills and enthusiasm for the game, which after all is the world's largest spectator and participant sport. However, your own soccer playing ability and soccer knowledge is somewhere between zero and very limited. But you do have great enthusiasm, a love for kids, and a willingness to learn on your side, all of which are necessary for a successful coach.

This book will build on those qualities and show you how to focus them on the coaching of youngsters. You will soon acquire the ability to organize a large group of children into practice sessions, to demonstrate and teach basic soccer skills, and to prepare your players for the upcoming season so that win, lose, or tie, everyone has a good time.

Here are solutions to all the various problems a youth soccer coach will inevitably have to tackle throughout the season. Answers to questions such as "How on earth do I teach heading?" and "How can I keep my players in position?" and "What can I do about that noisy parent?" are provided. This book covers the total experience of coaching youth soccer, not just what happens on the field. Information is presented in clearly illustrated, down-to-earth language.

The drills selected are suitable for the out-and-out beginner yet are based on those used by top professionals. More important, the drills detailed in this book work. They work because they have been tried and tested, by myself and other coaches, in both the United States and England. Many of them were developed specifically for American children at my summer soccer camps in the United States.

HOW TO USE THIS BOOK

This book is a valuable resource for both the novice parent-coach and the more experienced coach. Chapter 1 shows the coach how to teach. It outlines the principles of sound teaching method as they relate to youth soccer so that the coach can get the most out of the players. Chapter 2 shows the coach how to organize every aspect of the team so that the coach will get the most out of practice sessions.

Chapters 3–8 are concerned with the basic skills of soccer. Specific skills and techniques suitable for young players are carefully explained and illustrated. These are followed by a sequence of drills that demonstrate *how* the skills are taught. These drills begin with the first simple steps in the learning of a skill and progress to the more difficult stages. It is these *skill progressions* that will make your teaching successful. Be patient in the use of these drills and do not progress to more difficult ones until the initial ones are well learned.

In Chapter 9, principles of individual and team defense are detailed, while Chapter 10 covers the "set pieces," or throw-ins, goal kicks, corners, and free kicks. Both these chapters give sound advice for youth coaches without overcomplicating the issues. The emphasis is on showing the coach how to get the team to **do simple things well**.

Chapter 11 provides the coach with game drills in which players can practice the skills and techniques learned from earlier chapters. Again, the first few game drills are for beginners, but they become increasingly more challenging. Team formations for both six-a-side and eleven-a-side soccer are explained in Chapter 12, together with important tactics for team play.

It is recommended that the coach initially select the simple drills from Chapters 3–8, especially the chapters on juggling, passing/control, and ball handling/dribbling. These should be practiced and combined with the first few game drills described in Chapter 11. As your players improve and are able to perform more advanced skill drills, more challenging game drills should be introduced. Using the book in this way will assure maximum improvement in individual and team play, as well as player enjoyment. It will also make your experience as a youth soccer coach more satisfying.

The successful soccer coaching model (Appendix II) will help you to understand and prioritize the four main facets of the game, namely: winning the ball, keeping the ball, creating chances, and putting the ball in the back of the net (scoring). The Ten-Week Season Plans (Appendix III) are suggested schedules for your season for three age groups.

Once more it is emphasized that, although this book is aimed at beginning coaches, parents, and players, it covers *all* the basic skills and concepts in soccer, which makes it a valuable teaching aid for more experienced coaches and players. I hope you enjoy using it.

1
AIMS, OBJECTIVES, AND TEACHING HINTS

For the past 20 years, Americans have increasingly taken to the game of soccer, and for good reason. First, it is very inexpensive. You can outfit a whole soccer team for what it costs to fully dress one football player or erect a basketball hoop in the backyard. It is good, healthy fun, with lots of running, jumping, turning, and other movements that build fitness of the heart and lungs and contribute to a balanced muscular development for growing bodies.

Soccer appeals to kids of all shapes and sizes, so a big heart is just as important as a big foot. The injury rate is very low and confined mostly to occasional cuts, scratches, and grazes. It is a game that captivates the imagination of youngsters because, if they practice correctly and often, they will be constantly and visibly improving. It is a game boys and girls can play together, on equal terms, up to the age of about 14. It is a game that women have coached, and continue to coach, successfully, and it is a game in which men and women are equally inexperienced as coaches!

Before charging straight into soccer skills, it is necessary to set some goals for the season and to look at some general teaching hints. One would hope that the primary theme for the season would be:

EVERYONE HAS FUN
(Including the Coach!)

Fun can get lost within the hurly-burly ups and downs of a soccer season if you are not careful. But isn't *fun* the reason we all play? I also suggest the following more specific objectives, legitimate goals for every soccer team.

1. Improving individual soccer skills, enabling players to perform better
2. Promoting physical fitness
3. Developing good sporting attitudes toward competition

Sporting attitudes that should be encouraged are team spirit, team cooperation, determination, fair play, pride, and sportsmanship (which really means showing respect for opponents, referees, and teammates). The coach is solely responsible for setting high standards of sportsmanship. There is no better sight than a team lining up at the end of the game while their opponents file past and shake hands. Of course, each coach will have other objectives that can be added to the three above.

There is one additional point concerning "winning." When I coach youngsters, I like to implant a broad concept of winning in the minds of my players. I tell them that as long as they have tried their hardest and played their best, they are all winners, no matter what the final score. In that way, children can feel like winners every time they play. As players get older, especially when they reach the age of 12, they will be more able to understand win-loss records, league positions, etc. For children 12 and younger, it is important to de-emphasize the result and savor the experience.

TEACHING HINTS

A coach must be very precise with instructions, especially when dealing with children. If a coach asks 12 youngsters to "Give me a ball," that is exactly what he or she is likely to get—a dozen soccer balls. Of course that does not always happen, but it illustrates that there are certain dos and don'ts in the teaching of soccer. By the way, that is really what we are doing here: *teaching*, not coaching. Coaching is done with a squad of players who already know the basic skills and concepts of the game.

By far the biggest mistake that youth coaches make is that they talk too much. Children do not respond well to oral instructions. If you explain an action in words, they simply will not understand it. They will become uninterested and will turn off. Instead, give them five or six good demonstrations and then let them try it. Kids are fantastic imitators. Their brains are much more prepared to translate visual than verbal stimuli into action, so as a general rule *demonstrate* and *do*.

If possible, demonstrate the skill yourself. (This may require some private practice before the session!) If you cannot do this, ask a boy or girl on your team to do the demonstration or enlist the help of an older player. However you present your demonstration, make it *short*, *precise*, and of *good quality*.

Keep your players *active* with plenty of purposeful activity. This is especially important when the weather is wet, cold, or windy. Incidentally, kids love to play soccer in the rain. So instead of canceling practice and wasting valuable teaching time, simply structure the session so that players are moving at all times. Let the parents know that in case of rain players should bring an extra layer of clothing and appropriate footwear.

It is vitally important that a coach have a plentiful supply of soccer balls at each practice session. One ball per player is the ideal situation, but you should aim for at least one ball for every two players. They do not have to be $50 professional-quality soccer balls either; anything that is a size four and round will suffice. We've all heard how the great Pelé learned his soccer skills on the beaches of Brazil with a grapefruit! The more ball contact young players have in a learning situation the better. Use drills that give your players the maximum opportunity to kick, head, dribble, and shoot. (Examples of such drills will be given in later chapters.) Always remember to have a *high ball-to-player ratio*.

Once you have your players working, give plenty of *positive reinforcement* in the form of verbal (praise) and nonverbal (thumbs-up) feedback. Concentrate on highlighting the things they do well, not their mistakes. Reward good effort and good performance but don't go overboard so players expect praise every time they do something right. Of course, **the most effective form of feedback is success**, so it is important that the tasks set in your drills are not so easy that players get bored and not so difficult that players become frustrated. Drills should be structured so that every boy and girl has the chance to be successful.

Make drills objective in nature by setting targets for players to aim for. This gives the drills more purpose and the participants more urgency in their approach. It is also a good idea to occasionally pick out a group or player who is performing especially well to demonstrate to the rest of the players. Try not to pick out the same ones every time. Since there will certainly be different levels of ability in your team, be flexible enough to adjust your drills accordingly. Give the better players harder tasks to perform in order to maintain their incentive to improve. Remember that **success breeds motivation**.

Do not present too many teaching points all at once. If you do, the children will never remember them, let alone perform them. For six- to nine-year-olds, present teaching points one at a time. Pick out the most important teaching point and emphasize that first, and then add another later. For example, when teaching ball control, the most important teaching point is to get the body in line with the oncoming ball. When your players are beginning to do this consistently, give them the second major teaching point: to gently knock the ball off to the side and to get the head up. In general, **keep it simple**!

Remember the main points in teaching soccer:

- **Don't talk too much—demonstrate and do.**
- **Make demonstrations short, precise, and of good quality.**
- **Always have a plentiful supply of soccer balls.**
- **Use drills with a high ball-to-player ratio.**
- **Give positive feedback.**
- **For beginners, keep it simple.**

Other useful teaching hints include:

- Use your whistle correctly: Teach your players to respect the whistle—from the first session. **A whistle means stop.** There may be times when you need your squad to stop immediately (if someone gets injured, for instance). Don't confuse your players by using the whistle for any other purpose. To *start* activities or drills, "And go!" should be your command.
- Enforce safety rules: Never allow players to practice or play while chewing gum or eating candy because of the danger of choking. Make sure your players are not wearing anything (e.g., rings, necklaces, or earrings) that could be dangerous to other players or themselves.
- Always have a plentiful supply of water and give lots of water breaks.
- Tell your team from the start that when you call them they are to "hustle in." Just think of the time you can save! When they are gathered around, have them stand with their backs to the sun or any other distractions. Those with soccer balls should have their foot on the ball or have it between their legs. Otherwise they will be throwing grass around or trying to do their Meadowlark Lemon impersonation and might miss your perfect demonstration!

2
ORGANIZATIONAL TIPS

Being a soccer coach involves much more than merely coaching soccer. You have to be an organizational genius! Here are a few ideas that will make your job a lot easier.

Meet the parents. It is very important that you have a meeting with all the parents before the season begins. First, they are sure to want to know a bit more about their son's or daughter's coach. At the first meeting, introduce yourself and outline your philosophy on youth soccer. Hopefully your goal will not be to trample every local team into the ground but to let the kids have fun, make friends, play good soccer, and realize their full potential. After you have spelled out your coaching philosophy, the parents will know where you are coming from and will give you their support.

Second, you should delegate responsibility, a very valuable skill. Most parents will not mind being responsible for one of the many tasks that help the team to run smoothly: passing out the halftime oranges, being in charge of transportation arrangements or the first aid kit, being the game secretary (who confirms the games, referees, and the place) or the person in charge of marking the field . . . and the list goes on. Yes, you need help, and the more help you get, the more effort you can put into planning and teaching your practice sessions.

Furthermore, invite parents to help at practice. I have seen countless frustrated parents watching practice sessions from a distance who are obviously eager to help out. Most of your headaches at practice, especially with the younger players, will be getting small groups of kids "going" on a drill. Many kids will watch and understand a drill very well, but when it comes to transporting it in their minds to a place 30 yards away, they can be a little slow to get started. This is where a few attentive and helpful parents can be invaluable. They can assist small groups of players in getting organized and remind the kids of the major teaching points that you emphasized in the initial demonstration.

At your meeting, give out information sheets on the basic laws of soccer (see Appendix I). Ask parents to study them and offer to answer questions. It always amazes me how many parents think they know the laws of soccer after watching only a handful of matches. Unfortunately, while refereeing youth soccer, I have had to speak very strongly to some parents and even some coaches for verbal indiscretions. Referees are usually very approachable people and are normally quite happy to explain or discuss their decisions after the game. You should, however, make it clear to parents that this is your responsibility, not theirs.

Make sure parents know what equipment is required of the players. As far as footwear is concerned, young players need nothing more than molded rubber studs on their cleats. These are effective and comfortable for both wet and dry weather; flat-bottomed sneakers are virtually useless on wet or muddy surfaces.

It is also essential that young players wear the correct shinpads and the proper socks. There are several makes of shinpads made of soft foam rubber. These are comfortable and prevent minor cuts and scratches, but will certainly not prevent a leg from being broken in the unlikely event of a hard kick to the shin. Hard, plastic shinguards with a thin foam lining are the *only* type of pad that will protect against a hard knock on the shin. This type of shinpad cannot be secured onto the lower leg with an ankle sock. Long socks should be worn almost up to the knee to cover the shinpad, which should be pushed right down to the anklebone (where most accidental contact occurs). Keep shinpads in place with a "tie-up" at the top and at the bottom of the sock (Figure 2-1).

FIGURE 2-1: The Correct Way to Wear a Shinpad

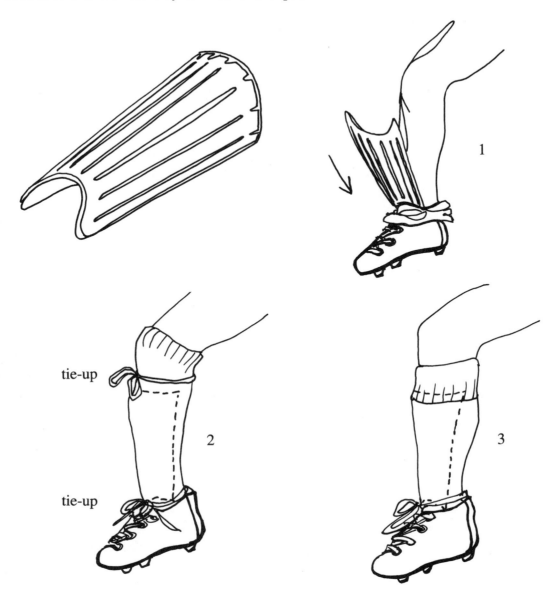

1

tie-up

tie-up

2

3

THE GRID SYSTEM OF TEACHING

The coach's most valuable organizational tool for practice sessions is the teaching grid. Grids are simply adjoining squares, 10 yards by 10 yards, in which small groups of players can practice. Without teaching grids you may soon find your players drifting toward every corner of the field, with you stuck in the middle.

Grids can be marked with lines, or better still, cones. A substitute for cones could be old soccer balls or basketballs cut in two and laid down, rounded side up. The advantage of using cones or other markers is that grids can be relocated to a different part of the field, thereby avoiding excessive wear to one patch of ground. You can also use the cones to alter the size and shape of the playing area. It might take one or two sessions for your players to get used to practicing in grids, but once they take to the idea, they will love it.

FIGURE 2-2: The Grid System

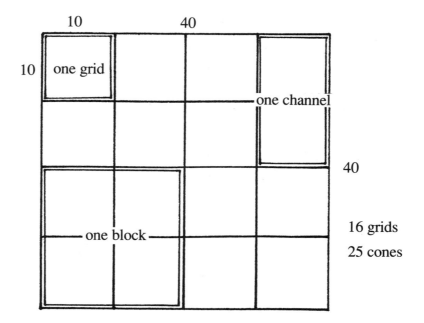

Using grids is very simple. They can be used individually, in channels, or in blocks (Figure 2-2). For example, when teaching chest control, bring the team in along one line so they can all get a good view of the demonstration (Figure 2-3). In this drill, the player serves the ball underhand into the coach who controls it with the chest and passes back to the server with the foot. The main teaching point, bringing the chest back on contact with the ball, is demonstrated half a dozen times. Players are then sent to the grids in pairs and told to alternate server and controller every five serves. As coach, move around the grids encouraging your players and correcting if necessary (Figure 2-4). When coaching on the outside of the grid area, always face inward so you can see the rest of the squad as well as the group with whom you are working.

FIGURE 2-3   FIGURE 2-4

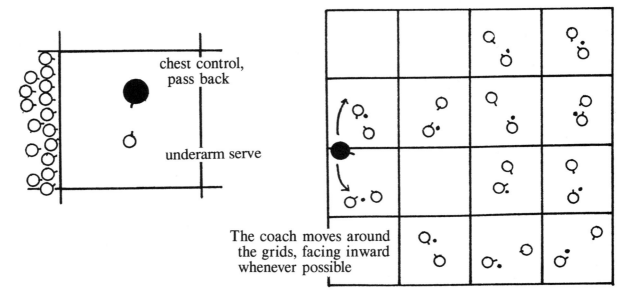

Players also should be instructed that if the ball goes out of their grid area they are to pick it up, carry it back to their grid, and continue with the drill. This helps keep the players out of each other's way and prevents minor disagreements. If you have a point to make to the whole team during a drill, such as the correction of a common fault or a small change in the drill, do not bring them all in; just stop them where they are and tell them about it. Again, this saves time.

PLANNING A PRACTICE SESSION

The importance of planning a practice session beforehand cannot be emphasized enough. Sit down for 15 minutes and think through what you hope to achieve from the next practice. Write down the skills and concepts that need to be covered in relation to the short term (your next game), and the long term (your overall teaching scheme). Taking a few minutes to organize the session on paper will save valuable teaching time out on the field. Take your planned session with you on either a clipboard or a small coaching card.

As the players arrive, get them to practice juggling and passing in pairs while you set your grids up, chat with parents, and remind yourself of your teaching plan. It is always a good idea to begin practice with some jogging, stretching, and four or five minutes of ball juggling in the grids. This warms up the team and tires them out a little so that while they are catching their breath you can demonstrate the first drill. This drill is designed to review a skill or concept taught in the previous session. You will often find that your players perform surprisingly well in the review drills because of a learning process known as reminiscence. These review drills also provide continuity between practice sessions.

After the review drill, move on to the main teaching themes of the practice. Introduce the skill or concept with a demonstration, bearing in mind the pointers described in the previous chapter. Once the drill is in operation, be prepared to adapt it as you see fit, depending on how your players react to it. If it is going well, run it a little longer. If it is not going well, either stop and explain again what is required, or modify it to make it work. If you see a common fault, stop all the players and point out the correct way.

Always give your players plenty of time to play. It may not always be a full game but players should get an opportunity every session to try the skills they are learning in a game situation. If time allows, finish the practice with a fun drill, perhaps one that allows everyone a chance to score on the coach. Then sit them down and congratulate them all for working so well. Praise the players who tried particularly hard, not just the best players. This is the time for announcements concerning future games, practices, and social events. Encourage players to work on their skills on their own during the week. After all, you see them only two or three hours a week, so give them their homework! The skeleton of the practice will look like this:

- Warm-up/stretching/juggling
- Review drill
- Main theme—skill and/or game drills
- Playing time
- Meeting

Once the basic skills have been taught, you should attempt to incorporate some form of passing, shooting, dribbling, control, heading, and juggling into every practice. To help you plan your practice sessions, I have included a suggested ten-week season plan for each age group in Appendix III.

SIX-A-SIDE SOCCER

Probably the most important decision that youth soccer coaches can make to improve the standard of play and enhance the enjoyment of players is to play six-a-side as opposed to eleven-a-side soccer. Ideally, children should play the six-a-side game until they are 12 or 13 years old.

A small-sided version of regular soccer can be found in every major soccer-playing nation in the world. Six-a-side soccer is played on a relatively small field with smaller goals (Figure 2-5). The laws of the game are exactly the same as in the eleven-a-side game except there are no offsides. For every squad of 16–20 players there will be two teams, split evenly or by ability, which can be changed weekly. For 7- and 8-year-olds, a 24-minute game is about right, with two 12-minute halves. For 9- and 10-year-olds, 30 minutes is appropriate, while 11- and 12-year-olds should play 36-minute games. Substitutes are required as there is a lot of running in six-a-side soccer.

There are several good reasons for playing six-a-side soccer with players 12 and under:

1. It is more exciting! Because the goals are closer together and there are fewer defenders, you will see many more goal attempts than in the senior game. This creates many more thrills and spills in and around the goalmouth.
2. Individual players get to touch the ball more and have an opportunity to be actively involved in the game. There is no point in practicing hard all week only to go out and touch the ball half a dozen times, as happens all too often when youngsters play eleven-a-side.
3. Players in six-a-side soccer also have more time and space in which to operate. Thus, they have greater freedom in which to express themselves, allowing skills and teamwork to fully develop.
4. There are no offsides! How can a seven- or eight-year-old boy or girl be expected to understand the offside law? Many parents—not to mention some referees—have difficulty grasping it.
5. Six-a-side soccer allows for a greater interchange of position than the eleven-a-side game. For example, defenders are free to go forward and attack the opposition's goal with other players temporarily "filling in" defensive responsibilities. This produces better, more versatile players and avoids the situation where a player gets labeled as only playing a certain position from an early age.

If in your community the eleven-a-side version of the game is used for players 12 and under, lobby for the six-a-side game. If you give it a chance, you will soon see a vast improvement in playing standards and in the enjoyment of the participants.

See Figure 2-5 on the next page.

FIGURE 2-5: Recommended Field Dimensions (in Yards) for Six-a-Side Soccer

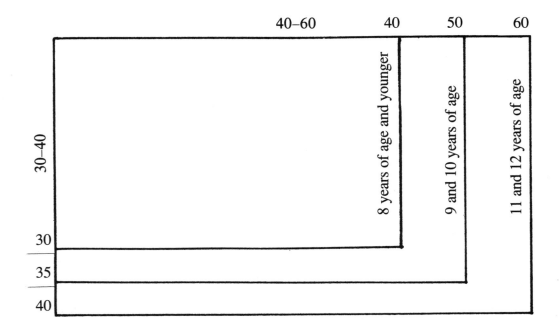

3
JUGGLING
AND WARM-UPS

JUGGLING

Juggling a soccer ball with the feet, thighs, or head is an excellent activity for both beginners and experienced players. First, it is a great warm-up activity. After 10 minutes of continuous ball juggling, the heart rate rises and muscles become warm and loose. Second, juggling helps to develop a "touch" for the ball and improves a player's close ball skills. Third, juggling helps a young player become more confident in his or her ability to control the ball. Confidence enables players to "relax on the ball," a quality that is vital in soccer. Juggling can be practiced individually and it can always be improved upon.

Players will develop their own juggling styles, but here are a few basic pointers. When *juggling with the foot*, contact should be made with the top of the foot or the laces. The leg should be relaxed and the foot should be flexed on contact (Figure 3-1). Balance is aided by holding the arms out slightly.

Thigh juggling is achieved by bringing the knee up so the upper leg is horizontal. Contact is made on the flat, fleshy top of the thigh. Arms should be out again and the body should lean slightly back (Figure 3-2).

Head juggling, probably the most difficult for beginners, requires correct contact of the forehead with the ball. The head should be cocked so that the eyes are toward the sky. Legs should be bent and should straighten a little every time the ball is headed (Figure 3-3).

FIGURE 3-1: Foot Juggling   FIGURE 3-2: Thigh Juggling

FIGURE 3-3: Head Juggling

The world record for juggling a soccer ball in the air is 16 hours, 27 minutes, and 52 seconds!

These three different techniques can and should be combined with other contact points such as the top of the shoulder, the outside of the heel, and the back of the neck. Of course, not all of these contact points are used in a game situation, but they are fun to practice and they add variety. One part of the foot I discourage using is the top of the instep, or juggling "hackey sack" style. Many learners use this incorrectly as an easy alternative to using the laces. Young players should be encouraged to learn the feeling of the ball on the laces because this part of the foot is frequently used for shooting and volleying.

Two qualities essential in all forms of ball juggling are *balance* and *rhythm*. Balance can be developed by maintaining the correct body position and using nimble footwork. To develop rhythm a player has to be relaxed and anticipate the movement of the ball. This takes much practice and the right kind of practice. Remember, **practice makes permanent**. If poor techniques are practiced repeatedly, they will result in a technically poor player.

Teaching Ball Juggling

Let us assume that you are teaching ball juggling for the first time to your team, and that they are all beginners. You have the grids set out and each player or each pair of players has a ball. The first stage is to teach them to develop a "juggling rhythm." Demonstrate and teach the following drill.

JUGGLING DRILL 1 (2 players to a grid, 1 ball each if possible)

Players start in the middle of the grid with a ball in their hands. The ball is tossed into the air about head high and allowed to bounce. Before the second bounce, players must move to the ball and tap it up in the air with their *hands*. Try to keep a sequence going. Players should stay in the grid.

Now show the players the contact area for foot juggling: the top of the foot or the laces. Invite them to press down on this area with their fingers to correctly identify the feel of that contact area. Now demonstrate and teach the next drill.

JUGGLING DRILL 2 (2 players to a grid, 1 ball each if possible)

Repeat Juggling Drill 1 except try to alternate between tapping the ball up with the hands and juggling it with the foot. Remember *not* to bend at the knee but to cock the foot up to meet the ball with the top part of the foot.

Players should now be developing balance, quick footwork, and enough juggling rhythm to try a foot-only juggle with a bounce in between.

JUGGLING DRILL 3 (2 players to a grid, 1 ball each if possible)

Repeat Juggling Drill 2 except use the foot only. Players should stay in the grid. More experienced players should try to use their weaker foot only and then alternate between left and right. Remember to give targets to players according to their ability.

Use the following drill to teach foot juggling without the ball bouncing on the ground.

JUGGLING DRILL 4 (2 players to a grid, 1 ball each if possible)

Players hold the ball out in front of them and drop it onto the laces, attempting to knock it back up to their hands. Have them do it once, then twice, then three times or more, without the ball touching the ground. Watch for beginners bending their legs too much and striking the ball with the shin or knee, a common mistake early on.

Again, some players will progress at a faster rate. Instruct these players to use their weaker foot or alternate feet every other knock. For those who find the basic drill too difficult, show them the contact point again and then redemonstrate the drill.

Thigh control is a useful skill that can be developed effectively through thigh juggling. Kids really enjoy this exercise and many find it slightly easier than juggling with the foot. Use these drills to teach thigh and head juggling.

JUGGLING DRILL 5 (2 players to a grid, 1 ball each if possible)

The ball is held in front of the face. As the ball is dropped, 1 thigh is raised horizontally to meet the ball and knock it back to the hands. If successful, try to make 2 thigh knocks in a row getting the ball back to the hands. Both the right and left thighs should be used and players must stay within the grid. Players then go on to try as many consecutive thigh juggles as possible.
    Remind your players:

- Make contact on fleshy part of thigh.
- Lean back slightly.
- Keep the arms out.

JUGGLING DRILL 6 (2 players to a grid, 1 ball each if possible)

The ball is gently tossed underhand just above the head. Players attempt to head the ball back to their hands once. If successful, they go on to try to make 2, 3, 4, or more consecutive headers.

Remind your players:

- Make contact on forehead.
- Cock the head back, eyes to sky.
- Bend legs and straighten slightly on contact.

After specific juggling exercises, players should have free juggling time to combine all the different elements of juggling.

STRETCHING EXERCISES

Most of the following stretching exercises involve a soccer ball. (If there are not enough balls, have the players imagine they have one!) Using a soccer ball during stretching gets them comfortable with it, and encourages ball familiarization. (You don't want your young players to panic when the ball comes to them in a game, so get them as comfortable with the ball as possible by using it in all activities, including stretching.) No doubt you can think of exercises other than those shown. Remember that all stretches should be done in a *slow* and *controlled* manner, not bouncy or jerky.

FIGURE 3-4: Soccer Stretches with Ball

left press   front press   right press   forward   middle   back

swing right   swing left   stretch right   stretch left   on heels   on toes

over   leave   back   collect

over and under   pass left   collect right

FIGURE 3-5: Soccer Stretches without Ball

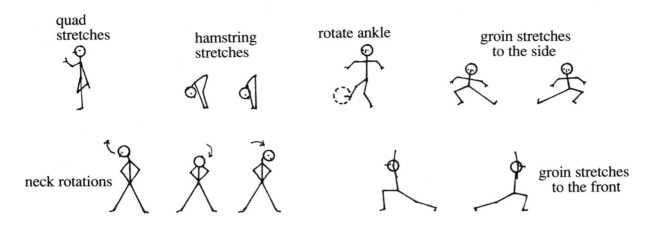

STRENGTHENING EXERCISES

Soccer is not a particularly rough game, but it is a game in which some contact occurs. Although physical strength in soccer is not essential, being strong can sometimes help to hold off challenges or tackles and can also help prevent injuries. Strengthening exercises like those in Figure 3-6 can be used in your warm-up sessions. Do not do too much strengthening work just prior to your skill drills; tired bodies do not acquire skills as readily as fresh ones.

FIGURE 3-6: Strengthening Exercises

OTHER WARM-UP ACTIVITIES

Juggling and stretching are just two of many activities that can be used to warm up your players at the beginning of a session. The best of these involve soccer balls in one form or another. Relay races are not recommended for two important reasons. First, they often involve sprinting or scrambling that for cold muscles can lead to pulls, strains, or torn ligaments. Second, with youngsters or beginners, if newly learned skills are put under the pressure of a race, they will usually break down.

Calisthenics can be used effectively for stretching and players often find it easier to stretch after a short period of jogging. Why not take your team and all the soccer balls for a little trot around the field? This is a good team activity and you can think of ways to make it fun (for example, by playing follow the leader). Give them targets to aim at on the way around and make the back person dribble to the front on your command. After three or four minutes of this, their pulses will be up and their muscles a lot warmer and ready for a gentle stretch.

4
PASSING
AND CONTROL

For the most part, passing and control should be taught hand in hand. Let us first analyze the basic techniques of each skill.

PASSING

The biggest problem young players have when trying to kick a soccer ball is using a *straight* leg. Both power and poise in kicking come from below the knee. Look at Figure 4-1. Notice how the player appears to be in total balance and how the kicking leg is bent at the knee, just waiting to be unleashed. This is the starting position for most kicks. The acceleration of the foot from below the knee creates a powerful foot-on-ball impact. This impact gives players the power to execute a variety of kicks. However, it is the precise contact of the foot on the ball that actually determines whether the kick will be chipped high, driven low, swerved left, or swung right. The basic passes in soccer are described in the next few pages.

FIGURE 4-1: The Basic Soccer Kicking Action

The Sidefoot Pass

This is the simplest and most widely used pass for short distances. It is easy for children to learn and very accurate, although it tends to be a little slow and predictable. Contact is made on the inside of the foot and ankle, with the foot turned outward (Figure 4-2). Keep the head down, kick through the middle of the ball, and follow through in the intended direction of the ball. As with all kicking actions, the body should be totally relaxed throughout the entire movement. Stiffen the ankle and foot *only* at the moment of contact. The overall action should look smooth, relaxed, and effortless.

FIGURE 4-2: The Sidefoot Pass

contact area for
sidefoot pass

The Outside-of-the-Foot Pass

This pass is slightly more difficult to learn than the sidefoot pass, but it is a more important skill to master because it is quick, accurate, and far less predictable. A pass with the outside of the foot can be modified into a "quick flick" for short distances or driven with an "away swing" over a longer distance. Contact is made between the laces and the outside edge of the foot, with the foot turned inward and extended, not flexed (Figure 4-3). Again, the head stays down and the foot kicks smoothly through the ball. The ankle remains stiff on contact, but the rest of the body is totally relaxed.

FIGURE 4-3: The Outside-of-the-Foot Pass

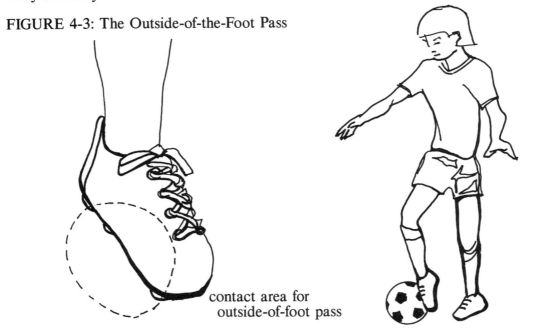

contact area for
outside-of-foot pass

The Instep Drive

Both the lofted version and the low driven version of the instep drive are used to pass the ball over longer distances. Once learned, this style of kicking can also be modified to produce a "chip pass" or an "inswinging pass." On a chip pass (illustrated on page 22) the ball rises sharply with backspin from the kicker's foot and usually passes over one or more opponents. On an inswinging pass (sometimes called a "banana kick") the kicker puts sidespin on the ball, which makes the ball swerve away and then back in. This pass is used to go around opponents. The approach for the instep drive is slightly angled, about seven o'clock (for right-foot kicks) as you look at the ball, and the nonkicking foot should be placed about 12 inches to the side of and behind the ball. Contact with the ball is made with the laces and the inside of the foot, which should be firm and extended (Figure 4-4). Once again keep the head steady, drive through the middle of the ball, and give the leg a complete follow-through.

Each of the basic kicking techniques described in this chapter has variations that make the ball do slightly different things. It is only through much practice, guided by sound instruction, that young players will learn to modify their basic kicking action. Being able to pass well in a game situation requires more than just sound technique. A good passer:

1. gives the ball good direction
2. gives the ball good pace (that is, weights the pass correctly)
3. times the pass to perfection
4. disguises the pass effectively

FIGURE 4-4: The Instep Drive

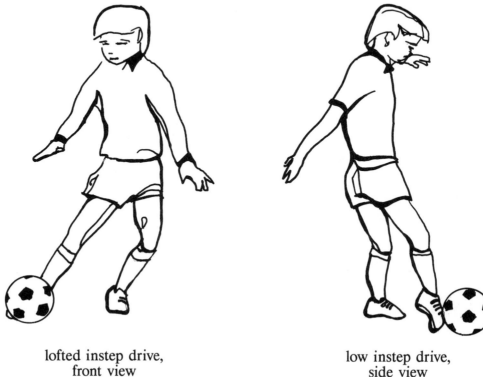

lofted instep drive,
front view

low instep drive,
side view

BALL CONTROL

Controlling the ball in soccer is as basic as catching the ball in basketball. Your team cannot do much if it does not have control of the ball. For a team to gain and maintain possession, players must be able to bring a moving ball under control and pass it accurately to a teammate. The ball may be approaching on the ground or in the air or bouncing unpredictably. A player may have plenty of time in which to collect and distribute the ball or may be under pressure from one or more of the opposition. Players need to be aware of the total situation in order to instinctively make the right decisions about ball control. Part of your job as coach will be to create practice situations in which youngsters can develop those skills and instincts.

As with all skills, there are certain basic rules to be applied in order to control a soccer ball. A coach should present these rules as follows.

1. Get in line with the oncoming ball. The first priority for the beginner is to stop the ball. This is best achieved by moving sideways to get behind or in line with the oncoming ball.

2. Choose a contact area on which to stop the ball. Whichever part of the body is chosen to control the ball, the decision should be made *early*. With practice this decision-making process will become instinctive. Different contact areas include the outside or inside of the foot, the chest, the thigh, the head, and the laces of the foot (Figure 4-5). These techniques will be detailed later in this chapter.

FIGURE 4-5: Contact Areas for Ball Control

thigh control

chest control

bringing the ball
down on the laces

inside of the foot

outside of the foot

3. Knock the ball to the side with the first touch and then look up. There is no reason why a player should control the ball and then stand still, and there is also no reason why the ball should be static once it is under control. Yet with beginning coaches and players we often see a player stop the ball dead, right between the feet. The player is static and will almost certainly have to look down for the next touch before setting up a pass or a dribble. By looking down, the player is temporarily out of the game. This increases the likelihood of that player being tackled and decreases the likelihood of the player being able to pass or move into space.

By using the first touch to knock the ball to the side, it is possible to keep the head up and set up the next pass or dribble (Figure 4-6). Note that the ball should be played to a side, *not forward*. Playing the first touch forward usually means playing the ball toward an opponent, giving the player less time and space in which to operate.

FIGURE 4-6: Control Ball to the Side with First Touch

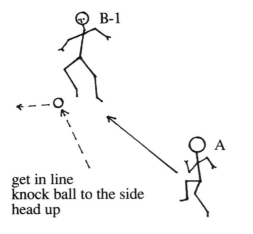

get in line
knock ball to the side
head up

opponent has to change direction
more time and space created for dribbler
new passing and dribbling possibilities

4. Relax the surface area on contact. Just as the oncoming ball comes into contact with the chosen surface area, relax or withdraw this part of the body to take the pace out of the ball (slow the ball down). This helps keep the ball within your playing distance. This technique requires much practice.

5. Do not allow the ball to bounce in front of you. A common mistake made by youngsters is to back off from the oncoming ball and to let it bounce just in front of them. This is one of the hardest situations in which to control a soccer ball. As a general rule, move *toward* the ball, not away from it. Take a high ball before it bounces or as it bounces (a half volley). Again, aim to knock the ball slightly to the side.

The following drills are designed to develop the skills of passing and ball control. The first few drills are for absolute beginners, but subsequent drills become progressively more challenging. After introducing and practicing the basic techniques through these drills, combine them with some of the simpler game drills from Chapter 11.

PASS/CONTROL DRILL 1 (2 players, 1 ball, 1 grid)

Players pass the ball to each other across the grid in pairs. Continue passing, using right and left foot. Ask players to demonstrate how many different ways they can kick the ball, and remind them to bend their legs when kicking and to move behind the ball to stop it.

PASS/CONTROL DRILL 2 (2 players, 1 ball, 1 grid)

1. Demonstrate and teach the sidefoot pass. Players practice the sidefoot pass across the grid in pairs. Practice with left and right foot. Follow through with the kick toward the other player.
2. Demonstrate and teach the outside-of-the-foot pass. Players practice the outside-of-the-foot pass across the grid. Practice with left and right foot. Kick from below the knee. Do not turn sideways. Remind players to relax when kicking and to move behind the ball to stop it.

PASS/CONTROL DRILL 3 (2 players, 1 ball, 1 grid)

1. Demonstrate and teach controlling the ball to the side. Player A passes the ball *slowly* to player B on the other side of the grid. Player B moves behind the ball and with the first touch knocks the ball to the side with the *inside* of the foot (Figure 4-7). Keeping the head up, B moves with the ball, stops it, and passes back to A, who controls the ball in the same way.
2. This is exactly the same drill as in part 1, except that the *outside* of the foot is used to knock the ball to the side (Figure 4-8).

FIGURE 4-7

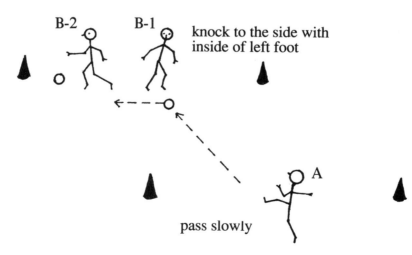

knock to the side with inside of left foot

pass slowly

FIGURE 4-8

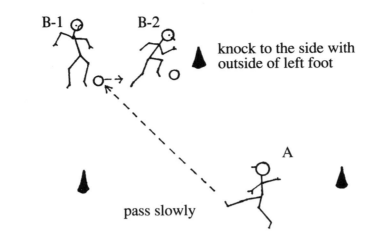

knock to the side with outside of left foot

pass slowly

COMPETITION! (2 players, 1 ball, 1 grid)

As with Pass/Control Drill 3, player A passes the ball across the grid to player B. As soon as B touches the ball, A may try to make a tackle. Player B must try to move with the ball to either of the cones on his or her line (Figure 4-9). Score a point each time a player touches the ball onto a cone. Reverse roles each time.

FIGURE 4-9

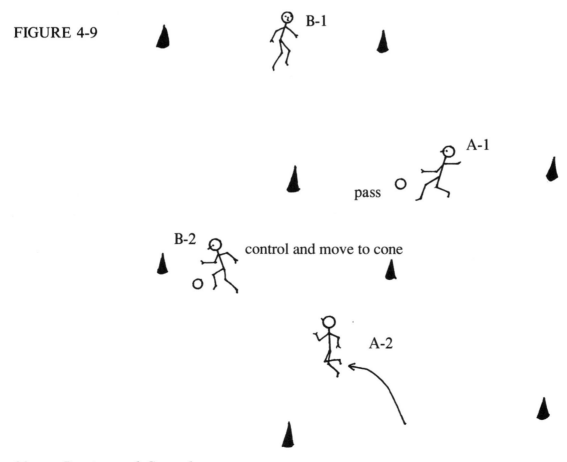

control and move to cone

PASS/CONTROL DRILL 4 (2 players, 1 ball, 1 2-grid channel)

If players are passing and controlling a soccer ball with some consistency and success across 1 grid, try some ground passing over 2 grids. Player A passes to player B across a 2-grid channel using either the sidefoot or the outside-of-the-foot technique. Players should look at the target, relax, and kick through the middle of the ball. In particular, watch for the contact area on the foot and the follow-through, which should be toward the target.

Note: Ball control will be more difficult in this drill because the ball will be coming in harder. Be aware of this in your coaching.

COMPETITION! (2 players, 1 ball, 2 grids)

Use exactly the same set-up as in Drill 4 above, but have the receiving player present a target by standing with legs apart. Players score 2 points if they can kick the ball through their partner's legs. Score 1 point if the ball hits either leg (Figure 4-10). See who can score the most points in 2 minutes.

FIGURE 4-10

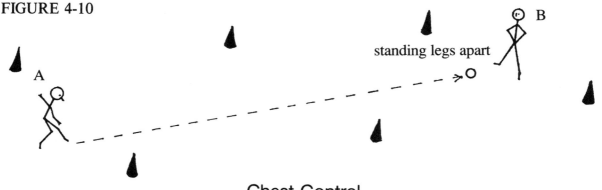

Chest Control

One of the most effective ways of bringing a high ball under control is to use the chest. If the technique is not taught properly, however, initial attempts will be unsuccessful and may hurt the young player. Get the players to familiarize themselves with the contact area by tapping the ball onto the area of the chest just below the chin. They can do this in pairs. Now move to the grids and try the following drill.

PASS/CONTROL DRILL 5 (2 players, 1 ball, 1 grid)

From about 3 yards away, player A serves a ball in chest high to player B (Figure 4-11). The serve should be underhand and soft, especially in the early stages. Player B controls the ball on the chest, brings it to the ground, and passes it back to player A. After 4 serves, reverse the roles. Gradually move farther apart. Remember to tell your players to keep their arms out and hips forward, and to pull the chest back on contact.

FIGURE 4-11

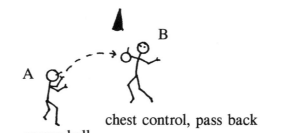

Thigh Control

PASS/CONTROL DRILL 6 (2 players, 1 ball, 1 grid)

Use the same organization as in the previous drill, but this time the ball is served in about waist high and players control it on the thigh (Figure 4-12).

FIGURE 4-12

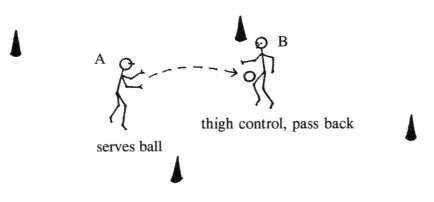

serves ball

thigh control, pass back

Bringing a Ball Down on the Laces

Bringing a high, looping ball under control is a tricky maneuver and is best achieved using the following technique. The player first uses fast footwork to get below the ball and plant the standing foot. The other foot, with the toe extended, is raised to meet the ball. As the ball drops, relax and give with it, bringing it down on the laces. With this technique, the head remains *up* as much as possible. Practice this skill with the following drill.

PASS/CONTROL DRILL 7 (2 players, 1 ball, 1 grid)

Player A on one side of the grid uses an underhand serve to toss a high, looping ball toward player B. Using the technique described above, B controls the ball and passes it back to A (Figure 4-13). After 4 serves, switch the roles.

FIGURE 4-13

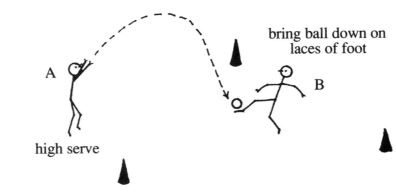

bring ball down on laces of foot

high serve

PASS/CONTROL DRILL 8 (2 players, 1 ball, 1 grid)

The aim of this drill is to get players to move toward a dropping ball that would otherwise bounce in front of them. Player A on one side of the grid is facing player B on the opposite side. Player A serves the ball so that it lands in the middle of the grid. Player B runs to the ball and controls it as, or before, it bounces and then passes it back to A (Figure 4-14). The receiver should control the ball to the side, if possible.

FIGURE 4-14

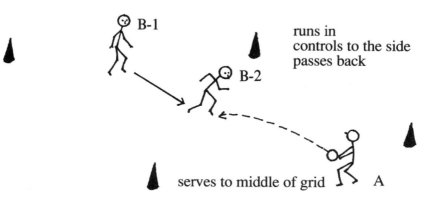

B-1

runs in
controls to the side
passes back

B-2

serves to middle of grid

A

PASS/CONTROL DRILL 9 (2 players, 1 ball, 1 grid)

In 1-touch passing, players interpass across the grid using a first-time pass. Start with soft kicks and move behind the ball. For a little competition, have the pairs compete for how many 1-touch passes they can make in 1 minute.

PASS/CONTROL DRILL 10 (2 players, 1 ball, 1 2-grid channel)

Players volley the ball to each other by dropping the ball onto the laces and kicking it away.
   Remind your players:

- Get in line with the ball.
- Cushion the ball.
- Do not let the ball bounce right in front of them.

FIGURE 4-15

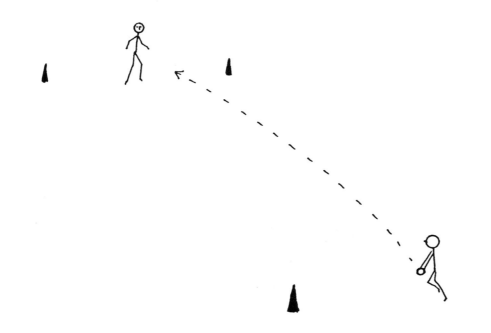

PASS/CONTROL DRILL 11 (1 player, 1 ball)

In this drill the player tosses the ball up in the air in front of him or her. The ball is allowed to drop. *As the ball hits the ground*, the player traps or wedges the ball with the inside or outside of the foot. As soon as the ball is trapped, the player looks up. Repeat.

5
BALL HANDLING: DRIBBLING

There is nothing more exciting in soccer than watching a great ball dribbler turn defenses inside out with fast footwork and the ability to do the unexpected. There is also nothing more basic in soccer than being able to dribble a ball efficiently and creatively. A good player is able to move the ball around, in front of, and behind his or her body, using all parts of the foot. Players need to build up a variety of techniques—including stops, turns, and fakes—to take on and beat opponents. Once they begin to develop such skills, their confidence will grow and they will create openings, pull defenses apart, and score goals.

This chapter introduces the soccer coach to all aspects of ball-handling technique. The practices described are enjoyable and effective in building dribbling skills.

DRIBBLING

The art of dribbling a soccer ball is a very personal skill and young players tend to develop their own styles. This should be encouraged. However, it is the coach's responsibility to teach the basic techniques of moving with the ball and to create practice situations in which good dribbling habits can be reinforced and individual flair allowed to develop.

In watching any of the really great ball dribblers in action, such as Pelé of Brazil, George Best of Northern Ireland, Diego Maradona of Argentina, and Johan Cruyff of Holland, two noticeable qualities are *outstanding balance* and *close ball skill*. These qualities are achieved by:

1. positioning the body over the ball (Figures 5-1, 5-2) and
2. using all parts of either foot at great speed

These qualities, combined with a blistering *change of pace* and an often bewildering *change of direction*, made those great players a joy to watch.

FIGURE 5-1   FIGURE 5-2

body over the ball
look beyond the ball

When dribbling a soccer ball, players can use the inside of the foot (Figure 5-3), the outside of the foot (Figure 5-4), or the sole of the foot (Figure 5-5). When dribbling, players should learn to look *beyond* the ball (Figures 5-1, 5-2). This allows the dribbler a greater awareness of the surrounding area so he or she can avoid the mistake of having "eyes glued to the ball."

As noted previously, a change in pace will often confuse defenders. This means that not only can an opponent be beaten by running speed but also by stopping speed. Stopping a dribble can be performed with the sole of the foot (Figure 5-5), or with the inside of the foot (Figure 5-6). The latter technique is a better method for stopping a dribble at great speed. Note that all the weight is on the back foot and the foot that stops the ball is fully flexed to effectively control the ball.

FIGURE 5-4

FIGURE 5-3

using the inside of
the foot to dribble

using the outside of
the foot to dribble

FIGURE 5-5

FIGURE 5-6

stopping the ball with
the inside of the foot

using the sole of the
foot to dribble or stop

Quick turns are another useful method of shaking off defenders. Use the sole of the foot to stop the ball and then drag the ball back (Figure 5-7). Having done this, the body can pivot either left or right. Use the inside of the foot to stop the ball and then drag it across in front of or behind the supporting leg (Figure 5-8).

FIGURE 5-7

quick turns using the sole of
the foot, then pivoting left or right

FIGURE 5-8

quick turns using
behind the body technique

The dribbling skills previously described can be developed with the following drill, which involves all the team members. A circular playing area about 15 yards in diameter is required and can be set out with cones (Figure 5-9).

FIGURE 5-9

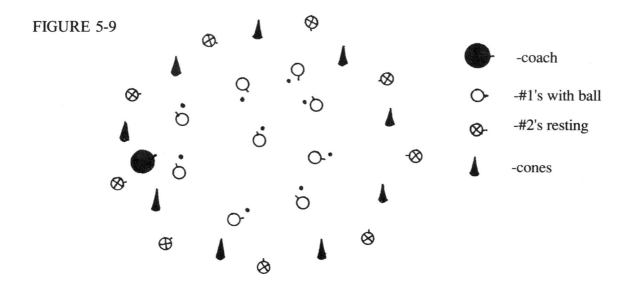

-coach

-#1's with ball

-#2's resting

-cones

DRIBBLING DRILL 1 (whole team, 1 ball for every 2 players, 15-yard circle)

Players pair up and number off 1 and 2. Number 1s take a ball and dribble around within the circle, while number 2s sit down and rest around the outside of the circle. Ask number 1s to use any technique to keep the ball close to them and to avoid running into other players. After 1 minute, repeat with number 2s. Now impose the following restrictions on their dribbling:

1. Use only the inside/outside/sole of the foot.
2. Use only the left/right foot.
3. Use any part of either foot.
4. Quick stop on the whistle.
5. Quick turn when instructed.
6. Move away from others and dart quickly into spaces.
7. Go slow, slow, then very fast.

Note: Use the techniques that have been described earlier and give half a dozen good demonstrations before allowing players to try it themselves.

Remind your players:

● Keep the body over the ball.
● Use change of pace.
● Use change of direction.
● Look beyond the ball.

COMPETITION! "KING OF THE CIRCLE" (whole team, 1 ball for every 2 players, 15-yard circle)

Using the same set-up and organization as above, number 1s dribble the ball around freely within the circle. When the coach gives the command "tackle," players attempt to kick other players' soccer balls out of the circle. Once a player's ball has been kicked out, that player must sit down on the edge of the circle. Continue until only 1 player remains with a ball, and then repeat with number 2s.

DRIBBLING DRILL 2 (16 players, 12 balls, 4 lines of 6 cones)

Ball-handling techniques can also be practiced using cones or markers to dribble around. Players are grouped into 4s, with each line facing a set of 6 cones (Figure 5-10). The front 3 players have balls at their feet. Before you start the drill, emphasize that this is not a race but a skill-learning activity. Players dribble in and out of the cones on the way out and return straight back around the outside. The dribbler then gives the ball to the next player in line and joins the back of the line. The second player may begin when the first player reaches the fourth cone. The following requirements can be imposed:

1. Use only the left/right foot.
2. Use only the inside/outside/sole of the foot.
3. Change the spacing or alignment of the cones.

FIGURE 5-10

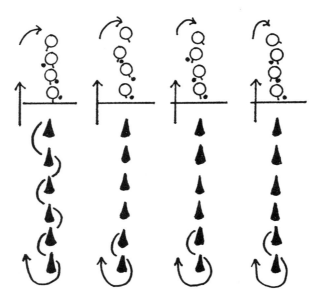

Beating Defenders with a Dribble

Always encourage your players to try new skills and dribbling tricks. You can teach them some, they can create their own, or they can learn from watching more experienced players. There are many ways of beating opponents with a dribble, but until those fakes or body swerves become instinctive they will not happen on the day of the game. Show players some simple moves and provide situations where they can try them out in practice.

One of the most effective techniques for beating an advancing defender is to use the outside of the foot (Figure 5-11). The dribbler throws his or her weight onto the left leg and then drives off onto the other leg, dragging the ball away with the outside of the right foot.

FIGURE 5-11: Beating Opponents with the Outside of the Foot

throw weight onto left foot

push off left foot sharply

drag ball away with outside
of right foot

Another successful technique is to fake a kick and then drag the ball back with the inside of the foot (Figure 5-12).

FIGURE 5-12: Faking a Kick and Dragging the Ball Away

aim to kick the ball

fake and drag the ball back
with the inside of the foot

If an opponent rushes in recklessly to make a tackle, the dribbler may be able to push the ball around or through the legs of the defender. The following series of drills will give players a chance to use balance and touch to "take on" and beat defending players.

DRIBBLING DRILL 3 (2 players, 1 ball, 1 grid)

1. Players A and B take turns dribbling the ball in a zigzag pattern across the grid and back (Figure 5-13). Players should practice using the inside and outside of the foot to stop the ball and move the ball across the body.

Remind your players:

 • Keep the body over the ball as much as possible.

2. Place a cone in the center of the grid. Player A runs at the cone (a defender) and cuts sharply past it (Figure 5-13). The cut should be diagonal and executed with pace and control. Repeat on the way back and then give player B a turn.

3. This time player A (defender) tries to take on and beat player B, who starts on the other side of the grid (Figure 5-13). Player A takes the ball over the opposite end line with control. Switch positions each time.

FIGURE 5-13

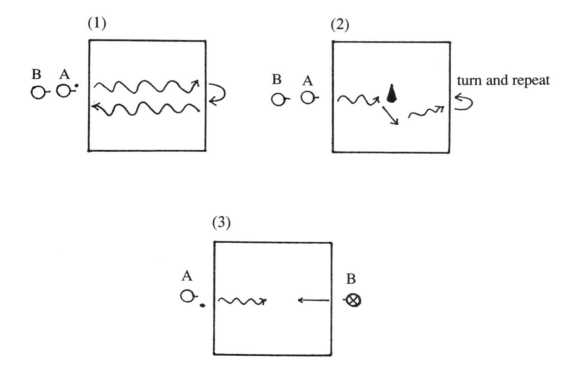

DRIBBLING DRILL 4 (2 players, 1 ball, 1 2-grid channel)

1. Two players face each other across a line between 2 cones (Figure 5-14). The player with the ball scores a point by pinning the ball against the cone at position A or B. The defender may *not* cross the line and can kick the ball away only when a score is imminent. Alternate starting possession of the ball.

FIGURE 5-14

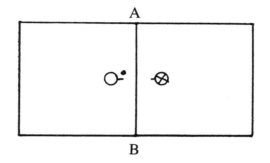

2. Use exactly the same starting position as in part 1, but make positions C and D the target (Figure 5-15). Defenders must stay in their own half of the channel until the dribbler crosses the central dividing line. If the defender takes the ball away from the dribbler, he or she may try to score at positions E or F. If the ball leaves the channel, alternate possession and start the drill again.

Remind your players:

- Use quick changes of pace and direction.
- Use foot, hip, and shoulder fakes to throw off the defender.

FIGURE 5-15

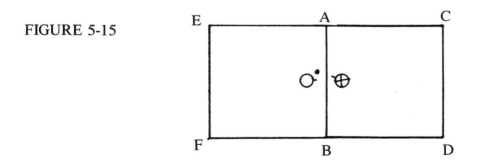

3. This time the player in possession starts on the end line and runs at the defender (Figure 5-16). The targets for the dribbler are positions C or D. Defenders must stay behind the central dividing line until the ball crosses it. If the defender takes the ball away from the dribbler he or she may try to score at positions E or F.

FIGURE 5-16

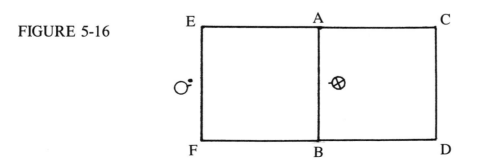

COMPETITION! DRIBBLING DRILL 5 (6–8 players, 6 balls, 1 3-grid channel)

Player A tries to beat the first defender with a dribble and then advances to the second defender. Defenders must stay on their starting lines. Dribblers must stay within the channel. They score 1 point for beating the first defender and 2 points for reaching the end line in control of the ball. When player A passes the first defender or has been tackled, player B can begin. Players who are tackled by the first defender go straight to the opposite end line. After each player has gone, the defenders turn around and the dribblers come back the other way. The defenders are then switched.

FIGURE 5-17

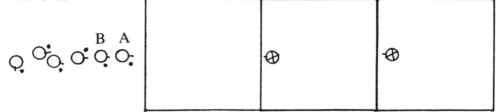

Receiving and Turning on the Ball

A skill frequently required in soccer, especially by midfield and attacking players, is to receive an oncoming ball, control it on the turn, and either pass or dribble up field. Many techniques can be used to achieve this, but the most simple is the *pivot turn* (Figure 5-18). It is important that players learn to do this because a team can achieve far more when *facing* the opposition than with their backs to them. On defense, however, you should ensure that the other team cannot turn with the ball and run at you!

FIGURE 5-18: Turning on the Ball—Pivot Turn

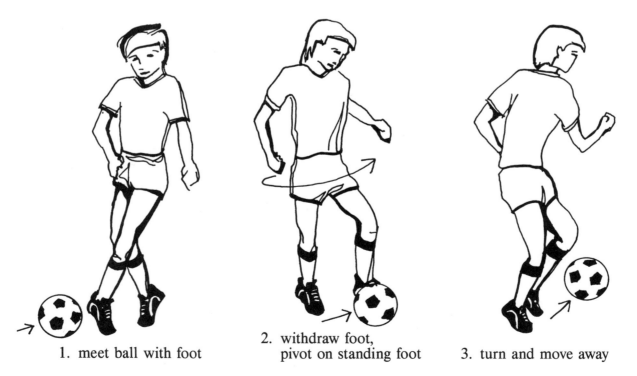

1. meet ball with foot
2. withdraw foot, pivot on standing foot
3. turn and move away

The pivot turn is a slick, effective technique when the receiver is *not* closely marked by a defender. If this is the case, a teammate should immediately shout "Turn!" (followed by the player's name) so that the receiver knows that there is no defender. Frequently, however, the player receiving the ball is marked closely from behind. In this case, a teammate should shout "Man on." A *shielding turn* should then be used to keep the body between the defender and the ball (Figure 5-19). Use either the inside or the outside of the foot to turn with the ball.

FIGURE 5-19: Turning on the Ball When Closely Marked—Shielding Turn

Use the following drills to teach receiving and turning on the ball. Both the pivot turn and the shielding turn should be practiced.

DRIBBLING DRILL 6 (3 players, 1 ball, 1 2-grid channel)

1. Player A at one end of the channel passes the ball (slowly at first) to player B, who is standing on the center line (Figure 5-20). Player B receives and turns on the ball before passing accurately to player C at the opposite end of the channel. Player C then passes back to player B, who repeats the skill before passing back to A. Continue for 2 minutes before rotating positions.

 FIGURE 5-20

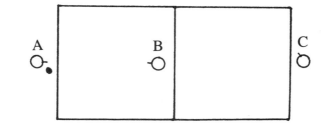

2. Use the same set-up as in part 1, except player B runs to meet the oncoming ball. As players become more competent, C can begin to move across the end line and call for the pass. Player B must respond to the call and pass accurately to the moving player.

3. Introduce a defender. Player C now moves just behind player B and becomes a defender (Figure 5-21). When the ball is played in by A, B must turn with the ball and dribble to the end line. Player C aims to take the ball away from player B and pass the ball back to A. Rotate positions every 3 minutes. Remove the center cones because they get in the way.

Note: Use this part of the drill only if players are performing parts 1 and 2 correctly.

FIGURE 5-21

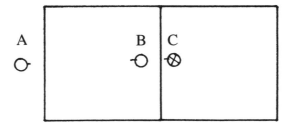

Shielding the Ball

When a player is closely shadowed, the ball must be shielded by placing the body between the opponent and the ball (Figure 5-22). This is the same principle used in basketball.

FIGURE 5-22:
Shielding the Ball

Keep the body between the opponent and the ball

DRIBBLING DRILL 7 (2 players, 1 ball, 1 grid)

Player A stands in the middle of the grid with a ball. Player B stands about 2 yards away. When the coach gives the signal, B moves around A, slowly at first, but then with increasing speed and irregularity. Player A attempts to shield the ball even though at this stage B is not trying to kick the ball. Once the principle of getting the body between ball and opponent has been established, allow player B to make a tackle if possible. Reverse the roles every 30 seconds. See who can keep possession of the ball for 30 seconds. Remind your players:

• Use all parts of the foot to move the ball.

6
HEADING

Heading is the one skill that really sets soccer apart from all other sports. Heading can be dynamic and spectacular, yet delicate and controlled. If you can send every one of your players onto the field confident and skilled in the art of heading, you will almost certainly be one up on the opposition. Once players learn how to *literally* use their heads, they add a dangerous weapon to their arsenal of skills. Players who can head aggressively, accurately, and intelligently can become at least 30 percent more effective than those who lack this vital skill.

The basic header in soccer is achieved by thrusting the top half of the body forward to meet the ball with the forehead. Contact is usually made just below the hairline, on the flat part of the forehead. The eyes should remain *open* until the moment of contact. If the eyes are closed, correct contact is unlikely. The neck muscles should contract, or tense up, when contact is made, thereby transferring and dissipating the impact of the ball throughout the rest of the body. If the neck muscles are relaxed the head alone will absorb the full force of the ball. Players should be taught to keep their mouths shut throughout the header to keep from biting their tongues.

One of the most important and difficult concepts to teach in soccer is getting players to "attack" or actively go after the ball in an attempt to meet it. This is particularly relevant with heading. Tell youngsters, "*You* head the ball. Don't let the ball head you!" (Figure 6-1).

The main teaching points for heading are:

- Keep the eyes open and the mouth shut.
- Contact the ball on the forehead.
- Use the top half of the body.
- Tense the neck muscles on impact.
- Attack the ball.

FIGURE 6-1: Attacking the Ball with a Header

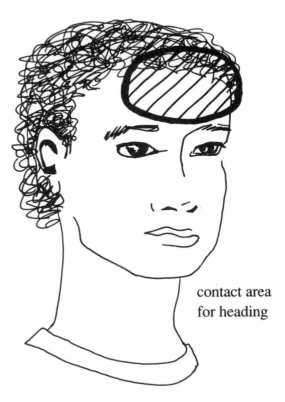

contact area
for heading

TEACHING HEADING

When teaching heading to youngsters, initial problems will almost certainly be psychological, namely, a fear of ball-to-head contact. By following the progressions suggested, even the most timid players will soon be heading confidently and enthusiastically. These drills are also of great value to the more experienced player or the one who has never been taught how to head properly.

If you start the practice session with "OK, team, today we are going to learn heading," you can almost feel the kids trembling as they approach. To take the pressure out of the situation, especially for the younger ones, get everyone to come and sit down around you (Figure 6-2).

FIGURE 6-2

everyone sitting (including coach)

Next, take the pressure out of the balls! There is nothing sillier than expecting absolute beginners to head a ball that is rock hard. So, before the practice, release a little pressure from the balls. Players will then be able to perform repeated headers and avoid the headaches and sore noses that could otherwise put them off heading for life. Once players become more confident and proficient, gradually use more highly inflated balls for heading drills.

HEADING DRILL 1 (whole team, 1 ball for every 2 players)

The coach sits down with the team. Players are seated in pairs with a ball between them. Show the contact area by holding the ball in your hands and tapping it gently onto the forehead. Then have the players do it. Next, repeat this action but begin to release and catch the ball. Then let them try. Ask them to check and see that their partners' eyes are open and their mouths shut.

HEADING DRILL 2 (whole team, 1 ball for every 2 players)

Have players sit opposite each other, about a yard apart. Player A holds the ball with both hands out in front, arms straight. Keeping eyes open, A simultaneously thrusts the shoulders and head forward while bringing the ball towards the head (Figure 6-3). This has the effect of heading the ball out of the hands and toward player B. Tell players to try to reach their partners without a bounce. Player B then heads the ball back to A in the same way. Sit them farther apart as the drill progresses.

FIGURE 6-3

A-1   A-2   A-3   B

The next skill to learn is heading a moving ball. Because more room is required, each pair can move to a grid of their own.

HEADING DRILL 3 (2 players, 1 ball, 1 grid)

1. Player A serves the ball underhand to player B who is kneeling about 2–3 yards away. Player B heads the ball back to player A (Figure 6-4). Switch positions after 4 headers.

FIGURE 6-4

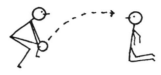

2. Player A gently serves the ball underhand and with two hands to player B who is about 2 yards away (Figure 6-5). Player B heads the ball back to the hands of player A. Switch positions after 4 headers. As the drill progresses, players A and B gradually move farther apart. (Note: The ball must be served in *accurately* in this drill.)

FIGURE 6-5

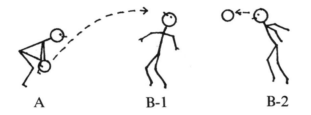

A   B-1   B-2

COMPETITION! HEAD-CATCH (2 players, 1 ball, 1 grid)

As in Heading Drill 3, part 2, player A gently serves the ball to player B but shouts either "head" or "catch." Player B does the opposite of the command. This makes player B think about performing the correct action instead of whether the ball will hurt his or her head!

Young players should gain confidence with Heading Drills 1, 2, and 3 before progressing to the following drills. If your players are heading confidently to a standing partner, you can teach them how to head high and low. To head the ball high, a player must get below the midline of the ball. To head the ball low, a player must get above the midline of the ball (Figure 6-6).

FIGURE 6-6

to head high,
get below the ball

to head low,
get above the ball

HEADING DRILL 4 (2 players, 1 ball, 1 grid)

Using the same organization as in Drill 3, player A serves to B, who attempts to head it high. Have players do 3 high and 3 low headers, and then switch servers. Make sure players are bending their legs and using the top half of their bodies, especially for the high headers.

COMPETITION! (2 players, 1 ball, 1 grid)

Player A, with legs apart, serves the ball underhand to player B, who tries to head it back through player A's legs (Figure 6-7). Score 1 point if successful. After 3 tries, switch servers and repeat. Player A then serves the ball underhand to player B, who tries to head it back over player A so that it is too high to catch (Figure 6-8). Score 1 point if successful. After 3 tries, switch and repeat. Instruct players to get under the ball, get over the ball, keep their eyes open, and their mouths shut.

FIGURE 6-7

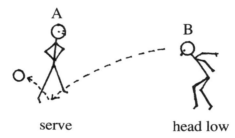

serve   head low

FIGURE 6-8

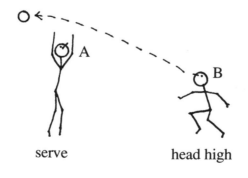

serve   head high

JUMPING TO HEAD THE BALL

To make a header in a game situation, it is often necessary to jump for the ball. Jumping for a header is a very important skill and should be taught fairly early. Heading a ball in the air is very similar to performing a jump shot in basketball. Both require an aggressive jump and the ability to almost "hang" in the air. Timing the jump and attacking the ball are other key elements in jumping for a header (Figure 6-9).

FIGURE 6-9: Jumping to Head the Ball

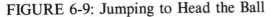

sink   lift   head   follow through

HEADING DRILL 5 (2 players, 1 ball, 1 grid)

Jumping for a header can be taught in the same way as illustrated in Heading Drills 3 and 4. Player A serves the ball high so that player B has to jump in order to head it back. Alternate every 5 serves. Be patient when teaching this drill—the timing of the jump is very difficult to master and takes much practice.

COMPETITION! (2 players, 1 ball, 1 grid)

This drill can be used to coach attacking headers. Player A serves the ball underhand high into the middle of the grid. Player B races in and attempts to head the ball into the goal below the head height of player A (Figure 6-9). Player A, acting as goalkeeper, can stop the ball with hands or feet. After 2 minutes, switch servers. See who can score the most goals.

FIGURE 6-10

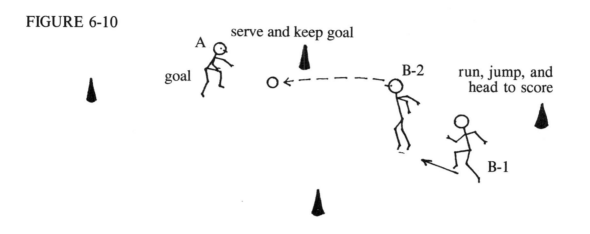

If your players have successfully completed Heading Drill 5, most of them will now be willing to put their heads to the ball confidently and accurately. If one or two are still a little timid about heading, they should continue to follow Heading Drills 1–5. The rest of the squad should progress to the following drills.

HEADING DRILL 6 (3 players, 1 ball, 1 grid)

In this drill, the player making the header must jump up—not forward into the player ahead (Figure 6-11).

FIGURE 6-11

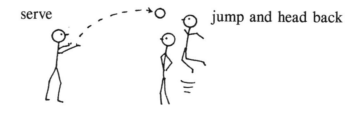

HEADING DRILL 7 (4 players, 2 balls, 1 grid)

1. Player A serves player B with a ball about head height. (B is standing in the middle of the grid.) Player B then performs a sideways header to the goal on the side of the grid (Figure 6-12). B then collects the header, leaves it back with A, and joins the back of the line. Change the server every 2 minutes. After 4 minutes, serve from the opposite side so players can practice heading to both the left and right.

Note: Players head to the side by turning the torso and shoulders just as contact is made. The forehead is still the correct contact area.

FIGURE 6-12

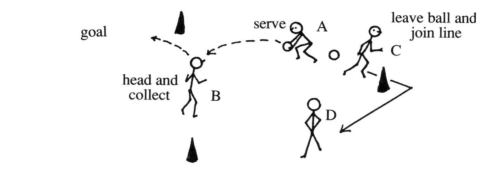

2. Introduce a goalkeeper. This drill is organized the same way as in 1 except that while A and C are serving and keeping goal, B and D are heading. After 4 minutes, change roles. Headers should be low and wide of the goalkeeper (Figure 6-13).

FIGURE 6-13

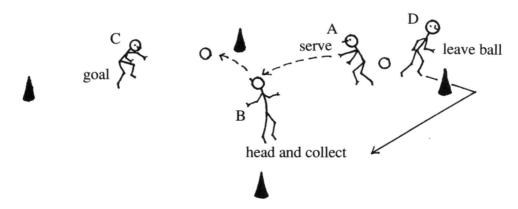

3. Players now try to beat the goalkeeper with a running header. Use the same organization as in 2 except players *run* in to head the ball (Figure 6-14). Player A should serve the ball just as B starts to run in. Attackers may even have to dive to reach the ball, just as in a game, but most youngsters do this quite naturally. Emphasize the starting and finishing positions in this drill.

FIGURE 6-14

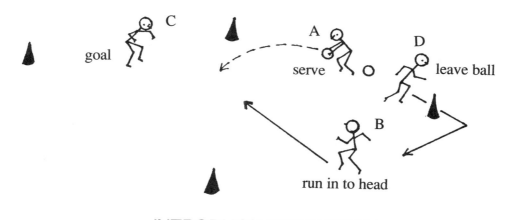

INTRODUCE OPPOSITION

After players become consistent in heading accurately and without hesitation, introduce opposition in heading drills. A skill such as heading should be tested only after it has been thoroughly learned.

HEADING DRILL 8 (4 players, 2 balls, 1 grid)

Players A and B stand on one side of the grid with a ball. Players C and D, on the opposite side of the grid, prepare to compete for a header (Figure 6-15). Player C aims to head the ball to B, while player D aims to head the ball to A. If successful, a point is scored. Players A and B must be able to pick the ball up without moving their feet. A and B alternate serving the ball. Change roles after 4 minutes.

This drill can be varied so that:

1. players A and B throw "neutral" serves high into the grid
2. player B tries to serve the ball to a target, which would be player C

Note: This drill involves dodging and marking as well as timing the run to lose the opposition. Note the starting position, with C and D on the opposite line from A and B. The only contact allowed between players C and D is shoulder-to-shoulder contact and then only when the ball is within playing distance of each player (that is, when they both go up for a header). Make sure players understand this rule, and you must strictly enforce it.

FIGURE 6-15

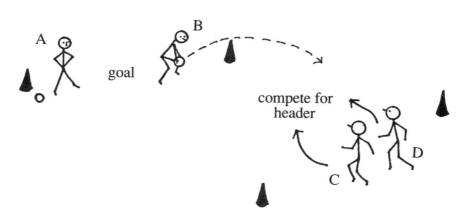

In the preceding heading drills, the ball is served in with the hands in a controlled fashion. This has been done deliberately because the players are learning skills and need a consistent serve in order to improve. Using a kicked ball in the early stages of heading development is unwise and impractical, but later on better players will need a more realistic service.

HEADING DRILL 9 (4 players, 2 balls, 2 grids)

Player A uses a shallow and reasonably gentle punt to serve the ball in to C and D, who attempt to score past goalkeeper B with a header (Figure 6-16). A/B and C/D alternate after 4 minutes.

FIGURE 6-16

Adapt the drill so that:

1. the goalkeeper can stay on or leave the goal line
2. players C and D are both attacking
3. player C is attacking and player D is defending (defender aims to head the ball out of the grid without a bounce)
4. players continue to play if the ball goes to the ground inside the grid
5. player A chips the ball in from the ground

Note: Attacking headers should be directed *low* and *wide* of the goalkeeper. Defending headers should always be directed *high*, *wide* (toward the sideline), and *long* (to give the defenders time to reorganize).

THE BACK HEADER

The back header is a very useful technique, but it should be taught only to players who have mastered the basic header. The player positions himself or herself below the ball and, with a backward nod of the head, flicks the ball behind (Figure 6-17). Remind players to deflect the ball from the top of the forehead.

HEADING DRILL 10 (3 players, 1 ball, 1 grid)

Player A serves the ball gently to player B, who backheads on to player C (Figure 6-17). After 2 minutes rotate positions.

FIGURE 6-17

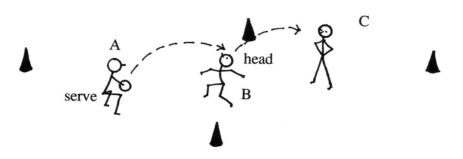

HEADING DRILL 11 (2 players, 1 ball, 1 grid)

1. Head juggling. Starting with a gentle toss, players A and B head the ball back and forth between each other. Remind players to bend their legs to get below the midline of the ball.
2. Double head juggling. Players A and B head between each other, bending at the knees and using quick feet to position themselves for the header. Player A first heads the ball straight up, and then heads it to player B. Player B repeats the process (Figure 6-18).

FIGURE 6-18

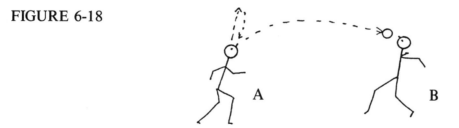

HEADING DRILL 12 (4 players, 1 ball, 1 grid)

To do figure-eight juggling, players head in the sequence A, B, C, D (Figure 6-19).

FIGURE 6-19

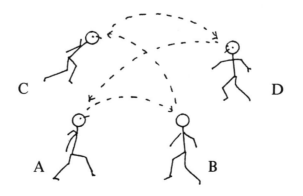

7
SHOOTING AND VOLLEYING

All the skills, tactics, and teamwork that you teach your team will ultimately lead to the shot on goal. The art of good shooting involves both skill and instinct, but an *aggressive attitude* toward shooting is equally important. Each player, especially the forward, must learn to take responsibility for shooting—and for missing. Never chastise a player for shooting unless there was clearly another player in a better position.

Shooting should always be the number one option. Funny things happen when you shoot: shots can be deflected into the goal; wayward shots can turn into brilliant passes; ground shots can get a lucky bounce; or the goalkeeper can drop the ball right at the feet of your forwards. You might even score directly from the shot!

Great attacking players always know where the goal is and they look to shoot at every possible opportunity. They have one thought in mind: getting the ball into the back of the net. That one thought keeps them running, chasing, and shooting until the final whistle. They take every chance for a shot as though it is the last chance they will ever get. In England these players are called "sniffers" because they are always sniffing out scoring chances. Not only are they in the right place at the right time but they make the most out of being in the *wrong* place at the right time!

Encourage your team to shoot whenever possible, and teach them how and where to shoot using the following techniques.

SHOOTING TECHNIQUES

Any kick that causes the ball to go toward the goal can be considered a shot. This includes all the kicks described in Chapter 4. The most effective technique for shooting powerfully on goal involves driving through the middle of the ball with the *laces* of the foot. This is very similar to the low instep drive (Figure 4-4). The head should be over the ball, the toe extended, and the upper body steady (Figure 7-1 below and continuing on the next page).

FIGURE 7-1: Power Shooting Technique

1. backswing—
   head down,
   leg bent

2. contact—
   head down,
   toe extended

3. follow through—
   shoulders steady

SHOOTING DRILL 1 (2 players, 1 ball, 1 grid)

Player A rolls the ball to player B, about 2 yards away. Player B, toe down, kicks the ball gently back to A, using the laces. Even on the follow-through the toe should be extended (Figure 7-2). The leg should bend and snap on contact. Repeat 20 times on each foot.

FIGURE 7-2

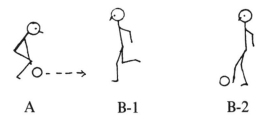

A   B-1   B-2

SHOOTING DRILL 2 (2 players, 1 ball, 1 grid)

1. Player A, standing over the ball with the nonkicking foot to the side of the ball, kicks the ball across the grid to player B, using the laces and emphasizing the extended toe on the follow-through. Player B repeats.

2. Player A stands a couple of steps back and slightly to the side of the ball (7 o'clock for a right-foot kick). Player A steps in and kicks the ball slowly to player B on the other side of the grid. Player B repeats. Players should exaggerate the good technique and *not* go for power.

As a general rule, teach your players to shoot the ball low and wide of the goalkeeper. Low ground shots are particularly difficult for goalkeepers to stop because they have to move their hands a greater distance than for high shots. When young players play in regulation-sized goals, they often score by kicking the ball over the head of the goalkeeper! This encourages the bad habit of shooting high. To avoid this, do not allow youngsters to play in adult-sized goals. Shooting wide of the goalkeeper usually means shooting to the corners of the goal, just inside the posts. Teach players to look up just before they shoot to check the position of the goalkeeper. Use Shooting Drill 3 (Figure 7-3) to practice these important teaching points.

SHOOTING DRILL 3 (3 players, 1 ball, cones as shown)

Player A shoots a stationary ball at player B, the goalkeeper. Player C takes the next shot as player B turns to face the shot. After 4 minutes, change the goalkeeper. Shooters should be about 15 yards back or a little farther, depending on the age and skill of the players. Vary this drill by:

1. asking the goalkeeper to take up various positions across the goal line
2. getting the shooters to kick a moving ball by rolling it gently away from them and shooting it before it stops
3. getting the shooters to toss the ball gently into the air in front of them, and shooting it on the second or third bounce

Remind your players:

- Keep the head over the ball.
- Kick through the middle of the ball.
- Contact the ball with laces.
- Keep the toe extended on follow-through
- Shoot low and wide of the goalkeeper.

FIGURE 7-3

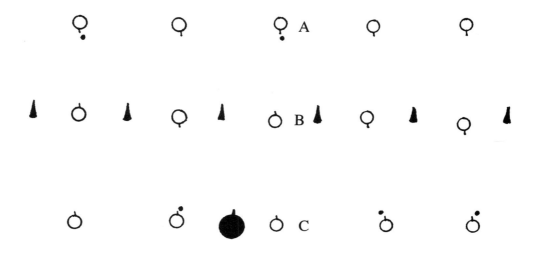

THE FAR-POST SHOT

A simple but important concept that will bring your team many goals over the course of the season is the *far-post shot*. When approaching the goal from an angle, it is better to shoot to the far post rather than the near post (Figure 7-4). First, the area of goal inside the far post is bigger than that inside the near post. Second, with a far-post shot any rebounds from the goalkeeper or the post will land directly in front of the goal. Near-post rebounds usually fall for a corner kick, giving the defense time to reassemble and reorganize. Use Shooting Drill 4 to coach far-post shooting and follow-up shots.

FIGURE 7-4

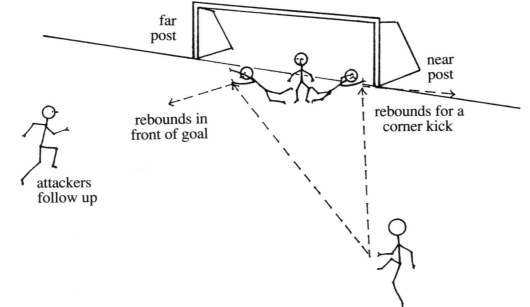

SHOOTING DRILL 4 (whole team, all balls, 1 goalmouth)

Players in the shooting line pass the ball firmly to a "target man," who is initially the coach (Figure 7-5). The return pass is collected and a shot is taken, using no more than 2 touches of the ball (3 touches for beginners). Players aim their shots inside the far post unless the goalkeeper leaves a large gap at the near post. Players in the rebound line run in, making sure they stay behind the ball until the shot has been made. Rebounds should be firmly kicked into the goal. Players in the rebound line collect the loose ball and then join the end of the shooting line. Shooters join the end of the rebound line. Practice this from both sides of the goalmouth. Depending on the progress of your players, allow a team member to be the target man and try some first-time shots (1-touch).

Note: If the goalkeeper saves the ball, it should be deflected or thrown out for the rebound line every now and then. This will keep the rebound line on its toes! For young players, use a parent or an assistant coach in the goal.

FIGURE 7-5

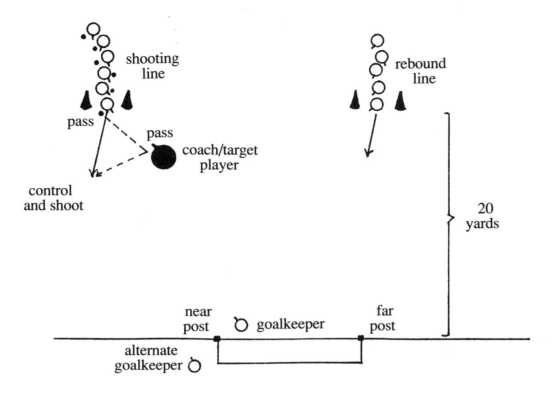

IMPROVISED SHOOTING

Every soccer coach has watched the unsuccessful goalmouth scramble in utter disbelief. The ball goes just about everywhere except in the goal! More often than not, the ball bobbles around the penalty area without falling conveniently onto the shooter's foot. Players need to *improvise* their shooting techniques in order to get a worthwhile shot on target. This could mean a toe kick (not normally encouraged), a back heel, a deflection off the knee, a desperate lunge—indeed anything that gets the ball in the back of the net. The following drill sets out to create a crowded goalmouth situation so that methods of improvised shooting can be practiced. It is a fun drill that involves the whole team and gives every player a good chance of scoring.

SHOOTING DRILL 5 (whole team, all balls, 1 goalmouth)

Organize your players into 3 teams, 2 opposing each other in the penalty area and 1 acting as ball retriever (Figure 7-6). The coach is positioned just outside the penalty area with as many soccer balls as are available. For 1 minute the coach throws, rolls, and bounces the balls into the penalty area in an indiscriminate fashion. The 2 opposing teams attempt to score using any fair means possible and improvising their shooting techniques where necessary. The retrievers collect and supply the coach with soccer balls. All competing players must remain inside the designated penalty area. Switch the teams around after 1 minute. Each team plays every other team at least once. As keeping score can be difficult, use parents to help.

Note: This drill is fun but can become a little frantic! Players should wear shinpads and kick only the ball.

FIGURE 7-6

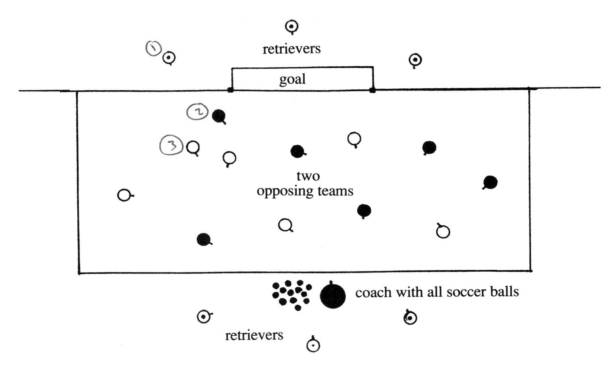

THE VOLLEY

A volley is simply a kick on the ball when it is in the air. A half-volley is a kick on the ball as, or just after, it hits the ground. Volleying is not confined to shooting—it can also be used in passing or flicking a ball on to a teammate (Figure 7-7). Whichever contact point of the foot is used, the player must get into position *quickly* and plant the standing foot early to establish balance. The ball must be watched all the way onto the foot.

Note: Coaches and referees should remember that there is *no law against high kicking!* A high kick can *only* be a foul if it is dangerous. At the youth level this law should be interpreted more strictly than at the senior level.

FIGURE 7-7: Three Types of Volley Kick

sidefoot
volley

outside-of-the-foot
volley/flick

straight volley
onto the laces

VOLLEYING DRILL 1 (2 players, 1 ball, 1 grid)

Player A serves the ball underhand to player B standing 3 yards away. Player B, using either laces, sidefoot, or outside-of-the-foot technique, volleys the ball back to A (Figure 7-8). After 5 serves, switch roles.

FIGURE 7-8

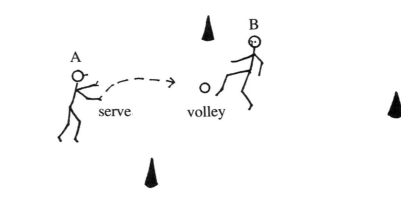

VOLLEYING DRILL 2 (3 players, 1 ball, 1 grid)

Player A serves the ball to player B, who volleys the ball to player C (Figure 7-9). Player C then serves it back to player B, who, in turn, volleys to A. Player B may use the sidefoot, laces, or outside-of-the-foot technique. Rotate positions after 2 minutes.

Remind your players:

- Use fast footwork to establish correct position.
- Watch the ball all the way onto the foot.
- Experiment with different techniques.

FIGURE 7-9

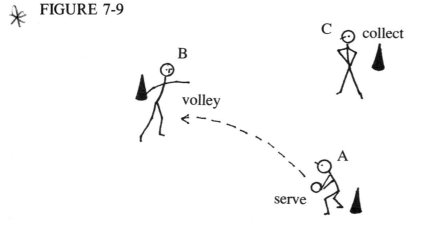

VOLLEYING FOR GOAL

One of the most awesome sights in soccer is to see a ball thunderously volleyed into the goal. To do this successfully, it is particularly important to establish a balanced position early and to keep the shoulders steady throughout, thus avoiding a pirouette-type movement (Figure 7-10). Practice volleying for goal using Volleying Drill 3.

FIGURE 7-10: Volleying for Goal

1. fast footwork to
get into position

2. establish balance,
prepare to plant
standing foot

*lift
leg high!*

3. plant standing foot,
eyes down,
contact ball on laces

4. shoulders steady—
turn hips on follow-through

VOLLEYING DRILL 3 (5 players, 1 ball, 1 2-grid channel)

Player A serves the ball in about waist high to player B, who volleys for goal (Figure 7-11). Player C is the goalkeeper. Player D then serves to player E, who volleys for goal in the same way. Player B then serves to A, and E to D. Change the goalkeeper every 3 minutes. Practice volleying with both the left and right foot.

Remind your players:

- Lift the leg high to get over the ball.
- Contact the ball on the laces.

FIGURE 7-11

8
GOALKEEPING

Some coaches say, "Goalkeepers are born, not made," but don't believe a word of it. Sound goalkeeping relies on practicing basic techniques. Good goalkeepers are superb technicians. They have to be—they are the last line of defense and cannot afford to make a single mistake. The perfect goalkeeper has no particular size, shape, or personality, which is why the position should be taught to the entire team. Occasional team goalkeeping sessions are a lot of fun and often lead the coach to discover the players who both enjoy and have the talent to play "between the sticks." It also helps the team as a whole to appreciate the responsibilities and special skills that the goalkeeper must possess.

It is wise to have two or three players who can do a good job in goal. Once you have identified them, use special goalkeeping drills to develop their skills. They will need individual instruction before or after the main practice session, but this will pay dividends before the season is over. Do not segregate the goalkeepers from the rest of the team—encourage them to play attacking positions now and then.

What are the physical qualities of a good goalkeeper? At the top of the list is a *good pair of hands*, or the ability to catch a ball. Second, a goalkeeper must be *brave* enough to throw himself or herself in front of a point-blank shot on goal, or to go down at the feet of an oncoming forward. *Strength* and *agility* are also definite assets, especially in diving or jumping for the ball.

The mental qualities of a good goalkeeper are represented by the three Cs: *confidence*, *composure*, and *concentration*. The greatest of these is definitely confidence. Without it, goalkeepers cannot perform to their full potential. They must have absolute confidence in their ability to save shots and to command the area in front of the goal. Some may have this naturally; others will have to be coaxed. Confidence *will* grow with improved performances, and improved performances will occur only if the basic techniques are practiced and mastered.

BASIC TECHNIQUES FOR GOALKEEPERS
Collecting the Ball

If one golden rule exists for the goalkeeper, it is to **get as much of the body behind the ball as possible** when collecting back passes and shots. This applies no matter how hard, soft, high, or low the ball is coming.

Even a ball that is simply rolling gently back to the goal must be collected by the goalkeeper with the legs together and almost straight (Figure 8-1). Many times a ball takes a bad bounce and can either pass between the legs or rebound off the knees of the unsuspecting goalkeeper if proper technique is not used, even in international games!

For a shot that comes in a bit harder, the goalkeeper should move quickly behind the ball and use the kneeling technique (Figure 8-2). There should be no gap between the front knee (the one on the ground) and the foot. The ball should finish securely in the chest.

For a shot that is coming in waist or chest high, the goalkeeper must move quickly to get the body *behind* the ball and, with elbows tucked in, take the ball into the chest (Figure 8-3). The goalkeeper should also "give" with the shot to stop the ball from rebounding away.

FIGURE 8-1: Soft Ground Ball   FIGURE 8-2: Hard Ground Ball

FIGURE 8-3: Stomach or Chest High Ball

With shots at or above head height, particular attention must be paid to the positioning of the hands behind the ball. Thumbs should be almost touching so that a "W" shape is seen (Figure 8-4). If possible, the catch should be made in front of the face (page 69), not over the head. This means that a jump is often required to attain the correct positioning. A one-footed take-off is an effective technique if this is the case. The nontake-off leg is thrust upward to give greater lift and to protect the goalkeeper from challenging forwards. Having successfully caught the ball, it *must* be taken to the safety of the chest.

FIGURE 8-4: Correct Hand Position for Catching a High Ball

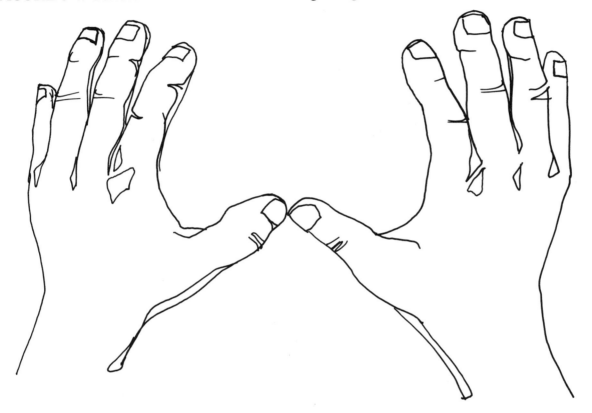

GOALKEEPING DRILL 1 (2 players, 1 ball, 1 grid)

Players work with a partner, about 8 yards apart. Practice the techniques of collecting a soccer ball by rolling or throwing the ball from the hands. Players should not kick the ball to their partners at this stage. Work through the techniques in sequence, from the rolling ball, to the waist/chest high ball, to the ball at or above head height. In a whole team session, spend 2 minutes on each skill. Spend a much longer time with the regular goalkeepers until the techniques are mastered.

Shot Stopping

A goalkeeper should adopt the "position of readiness" when preparing to save a shot (Figure 8-5). The weight is forward and on the balls of the feet, and the hands are open and half raised. From this balanced position the goalkeeper can move quickly to block the ball in any direction.

When learning to dive for the ball, many youngsters make the mistake of "belly flopping" with the stomach downward. This position is inefficient and can be painful if the goalkeeper lands on the ball or an elbow and knocks the wind out of himself or herself. The correct diving position for a goalkeeper is with the body sideways (Figure 8-6). This ensures that:

1. the greatest possible body area is available for stopping the ball
2. both arms and hands are free to reach for the ball
3. the head is facing the oncoming ball at all times and does not need to be turned

This is the most efficient technique whether going full stretch for a wide ball (Figure 8-7) or dropping on a ball close to the feet (Figure 8-8).

The *first* priority for a goalkeeper is to prevent the ball from crossing the goal line. Deflecting the ball for a corner is fine, but if the ball is within reach, a flying catch is preferred. If the goalkeeper opts for a catch, the ball should *always* finish in the chest. If the ball is accidently fumbled, every attempt must be made to scramble and dive on the ball.

FIGURE 8-5: Position of Readiness for Diving

FIGURE 8-6: Sideways Dive

FIGURE 8-7

diving sideways at full stretch
to deflect the ball around goalpost

FIGURE 8-8

dropping on the ball with
sideways body position

GOALKEEPING DRILL 2 (2 players, 1 ball, 1 grid)

1. If possible, move grids to an area with thick grass. From a kneeling position, the goalkeeper holds the ball securely against the chest and practices falling onto the side, both to the left and right (Figure 8-9). Repeat this action with the goalkeeper holding the ball in front of or above the head. As he or she begins to fall sideways, the ball is taken to the chest. Do not allow the goalkeeper to roll onto the back. Change goalkeepers after 2 minutes.

FIGURE 8-9

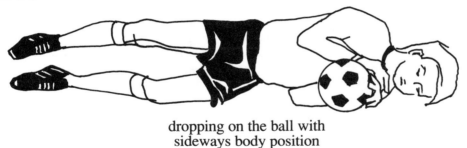

hold ball
in chest

fall to side

hold ball high

bring ball to chest
while falling

2. This time the kneeling goalkeeper receives a gentle underhand serve from a partner who stands about 3 yards away (Figure 8-10). The serve should go directly to the goalkeeper at first, and then increasingly to the side until the goalkeeper is taking the ball in a kneeling dive. Change goalkeepers after 3 minutes.

FIGURE 8-10

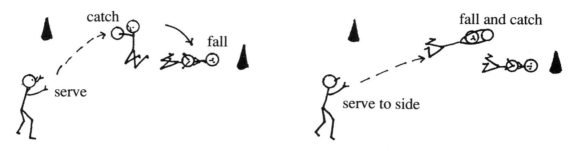

3. Repeat the previous drill, except this time the serves should be faster and more challenging. The goalkeeper will soon be diving correctly without thinking about technique. At this stage, some bouncing serves should be thrown; these are particularly difficult to stop and need to be practiced.
4. Start the goalkeeper in a low crouch/squat position (Figure 8-11). Use the underhand serve and make sure the goalkeeper finishes with the ball in the chest.

FIGURE 8-11

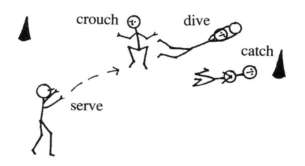

5. Start the goalkeeper in the position of readiness (Figure 8-5). The server moves back to the other side of the grid and uses a half-volley kick at, or just to the side of, the goalkeeper. (A half-volley can be achieved by dropping the ball and kicking it with the laces as it hits the ground.) If a half-volley is too difficult for your players, a regular kick from the ground can be used (Figure 8-12).
Note: It is not necessary to complete steps 1–5 in one session. The time spent on each stage depends on the age and ability of the players.

FIGURE 8-12

Distributing the Ball

Although the goalkeeper is truly the last line of defense, he or she is also the first line of attack. Many attacking moves can be set up by a quick-thinking goalkeeper who uses an accurate throw to the wing or a solid kick down the middle. Remember that the goalkeeper can take only four steps once he or she has established possession of the ball with the hands.

The goalkeeper can use an *underhand roll* (10-pin bowling style) to pass the ball quickly and accurately to a nearby teammate (Figure 8-13). To pass the ball farther, a low *javelin pass* is used. This is similar to a length-of-the-court pass in basketball, except the ball is pushed away much lower (Figure 8-14). The javelin pass is useful because it gets to the target quickly and it arrives at the player's feet. For long clearances or when attackers are in the way, a *kick or overhand throw* is used (Figure 8-15). In the latter, the arm is straight throughout the movement and follows an overhand bowling-type action.

FIGURE 8-13: The Roll Out

FIGURE 8-14: The Javelin Pass

FIGURE 8-15: The Overarm Throw

The easiest form of kicked clearance is the straightforward *punt* (Figure 8-16). Ideally the goalkeeper should be able to punt with both the left and right foot. The ball is dropped onto the foot, not tossed in the air, and the foot is slightly extended. The half-volley kicked clearance is more difficult but results in a lower trajectory. In youth soccer, it is important to **put the ball wide or down the sidelines**. This presents the least danger to the goal, particularly if the goalkeeper does not have a strong clearance. It also leaves more space down the flanks for your team to build an attack.

FIGURE 8-16: The Punted Clearance

GOALKEEPING DRILL 3 (2 players, 1 ball)

1. Work across one grid. Have players roll the ball underhand to their partners.
2. Work across a 2-grid channel. Have players throw the ball to each other using the javelin pass technique. Work on accuracy and making the ball arrive at the player's feet. The farther out the front foot, the lower the pass delivery.
3. Move players farther apart and practice both the overhand throw and the punt.
4. Allow players to use any part of the open field to practice distribution techniques. Make the receiver move so the goalkeeper has to hit a moving target.

Goalkeeping Angles

Correct positioning in front of the goal is a vital factor in shot stopping. *Not* having to dive at every shot on goal is a sure sign of a goalkeeper who has "got the angles right." When the ball is close to the goal, the goalkeeper should constantly be adjusting his or her position to ensure equal coverage for both sides of the goal (Figure 8-17).

FIGURE 8-17

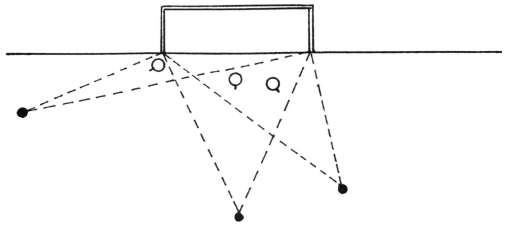

GOALKEEPING DRILL 4 (2 players, 1 ball, 1 goal)

Player A, the goalkeeper, is approximately 2 yards off the goal line. Player B, the shooter, is about 15 yards away with a ball. Player B dribbles on an arc in front of the goal (Figure 8-18), forcing the goalkeeper to adjust his or her position so that both sides of the goal are covered. When B stops, A stops immediately to check that the correct positioning has been achieved. After 1 minute of stopping and checking, player B can shoot when a positional weakness is spotted. After 2 minutes of shooting, switch roles.

Note: This drill is suitable only for experienced players or for the coach and the goalkeeper.

FIGURE 8-18

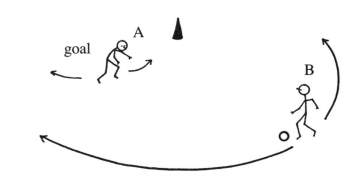

Narrowing the Angle of Shots

By advancing a few steps toward the ball, a goalkeeper represents a large obstacle to the shooter (Figure 8-19). This is called *narrowing the angle* of shots on goal and is an effective technique in shot stopping. Care should be taken that:

1. both sides of the goal are still covered
2. the advance is fast and a balanced position is reestablished before the shot is made
3. the goalkeeper does not advance too far and become vulnerable to a chip shot

FIGURE 8-19: Narrowing the Angle of Shots on Goal

goalkeeper on goal line

goalkeeper advances,
presents larger obstacle

Use Goalkeeping Drill 5 to practice narrowing angles.

GOALKEEPING DRILL 5 (6–10 players, 5 balls, 1 goalmouth)

The goalkeeper starts on the goal line. From a central position 30 yards out, attackers run at the goal and take a shot from a point anywhere in front of the two cones located 15 yards from the goal line. Attackers may approach the goal from any angle. Switch goalkeepers every 10 shots.

FIGURE 8-20

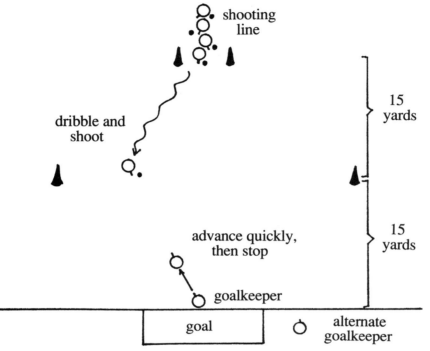

Punching the Ball Clear

When faced with high shots or crosses (balls kicked high across the goal) the goalkeeper must show complete confidence. A *two-handed catch* should always be the first option. If the goalkeeper is not sure of making a safe catch, a *two-fisted punch* is the next best option (Figure 8-21). This should be performed aggressively with the ball traveling long, high, and wide of the goalmouth. A punch is a particularly effective technique to use when conditions are wet and slippery or when there are too many players competing for the ball.

FIGURE 8-21

two-fisted punch
through middle of ball

Dealing with Crosses

When a goalkeeper decides to go for a high cross ball (page 69), he or she should *decide early* and make a *late but fast* run toward the ball. This way the goalkeeper is not jumping up among other players. In addition, the goalkeeper must *call for the ball* so the defenders can get out of the way and fall behind to cover. The call must be loud and positive, such as "Keeper's ball!"

9
BALL WINNING
AND DEFENSE

In youth soccer, less emphasis should be placed on the defensive aspects of the game than on offense. The coach's primary responsibility is to develop attacking skills (dribbling, passing, ball control, shooting, and heading). I subscribe to the coaching adage that "Attack is the best form of defense." Defensive concepts and tactics tend to confuse younger players and should be kept to a minimum. Defensive skills and tactics can be taught to players over 10. Teach only basic concepts to younger players; they will develop defensive skills naturally.

BALL WINNING

Ball winning involves an important attitude that must be developed with young players in a healthy and competitive manner. To be successful, a team must have the desire and the ability to win possession of the ball. To win the loose ball, a player must get to the ball first. This means *running to* the ball, not standing still or backing off, a common mistake youngsters make. When a player is in a position to challenge for the ball, some contact with opponents is inevitable. (Soccer *is* a contact game.) Some kids relish the contact aspect of the game; others shy away from it.

The following drill will teach your squad how to make a *fair* but *positive* challenge for the ball. These three simple rules can help players learn to handle contact situations safely and within the laws of the game:

- Make side-to-side, shoulder-to-shoulder contact only.
- Keep elbows in.
- Play only the ball—any foot contact on an opponent is a foul.

BALL-WINNING DRILL 1 (10 players, all balls, ½ field)

The coach stands 20 yards from the goal with all the soccer balls. Four attackers stand approximately 40 yards from the goal across from four defensive players (Figure 9-1). When the coach throws the first ball out, players at the front of each line compete for the ball. Defenders aim to pass or dribble the ball back to the coach, while attackers aim to score past the goalkeeper. Players rejoin the opposite line next time up. When serving, try to increase the confidence of the shy players. Vary the position of the cones across the field and vary the type of serve given (ground, bouncing, or high balls). Switch goalkeepers about every four minutes.

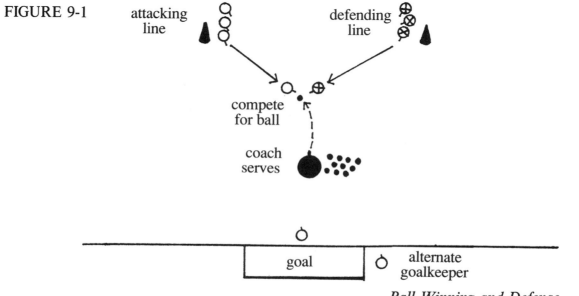

FIGURE 9-1

attacking line

defending line

compete for ball

coach serves

goal

alternate goalkeeper

Tackling

Once players develop a determined ball-winning attitude, they will make more successful tackles. As noted previously, young players do not need to know the intricate details of how and when to tackle. There is no special skill involved in performing a basic foot tackle. Just tell your players to keep their eyes on the ball, to kick through the middle of the ball, and to go into a tackle with 100 percent commitment, not hanging back. This increases the chances of winning the tackle and decreases the chances of getting hurt. Make sure that players kick *only* the ball when tackling. Be very strict with any players who are reckless or dangerous in their tackling.

A defender's first priority when making a tackle is to dispossess or kick the ball away from the player with the ball. A player can use many different kicks to achieve this objective, but he or she should try to stay on his or her feet. If a standing *block* tackle is not possible, a *sliding* tackle can be used to kick the ball away (Figure 9-2). If the slide is done in a controlled fashion with the foot positioned behind the ball, the tackler can even come away with the ball (Figure 9-3). The attacker, in effect, will stumble over the ball.

FIGURE 9-2: Dispossessing an Opponent with a Sliding Tackle

FIGURE 9-3: Winning the Ball in Tackle

DEFENSIVE ASPECTS

The basic defensive principles outlined in this section are for soccer coaches at any level. Teach them to younger players gradually and with discretion.

Team Defense

The most important concept of team defense is to **get behind the ball the moment it is lost to the other team**. Teach your players that they should all *attack* when they've got the ball, and all *defend* when the opponent has the ball. The quickest way to recover behind the ball is to simply run straight back toward your own goal. The forwards will not need to recover all the way behind the ball because they will probably be marking opposing defenders.

The other major principle in team defense is to protect the *defensive danger zone* or the area in front of goal where most goals are scored (Figure 9-4). If this zone is defended effectively, the goal will be under far less pressure. To do this your players must:

1. keep the ball out of the danger zone
2. clear the ball quickly and efficiently if the ball does enter
3. not allow themselves to be outnumbered near the goal

Points 1 and 2 will be expanded upon in the section on individual defense. Point 3 can be achieved if the defense recovers *quickly* behind the ball and into the defensive danger zone. Team defense also involves pressuring attackers in possession of the ball and covering for defenders if they get beaten with a dribble. Opponents must never be allowed a clear run on goal. The player with the ball is the most important and should always be marked tightly. If there is one defender and two or more attackers, the defender should *always* take the player with the ball.

FIGURE 9-4: The Defensive Danger Zone

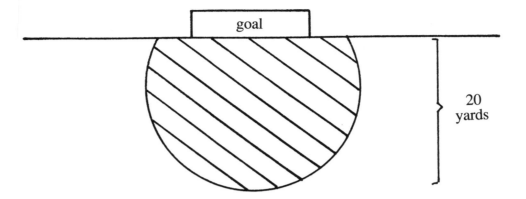

Individual Defense

The following teaching points, although relatively simple, can be difficult for young players. Be selective in your use of them.

After recovering behind the ball, defenders should immediately *mark-up* or *track* all unguarded attacking players. This is achieved by getting *goal side* of the player they are marking (Figure 9-5), whether or not that player has the ball. To get goal side, the defender should stand roughly on a line between the attacker and the goal.

If the player does not have the ball, the defender should stay goal side and follow this simple rule: **the closer the ball, the tighter the marking**. If the ball is very close, the defender should be slightly more than one arm's length away from the attacker; any closer and the defender can be turned easily. When the ball is on the other side of the field, the defender should drop about 10–15 feet away (Figure 9-6). Players should use peripheral vision to follow both the ball and the player being marked.

FIGURE 9-5: Goal Side Marking

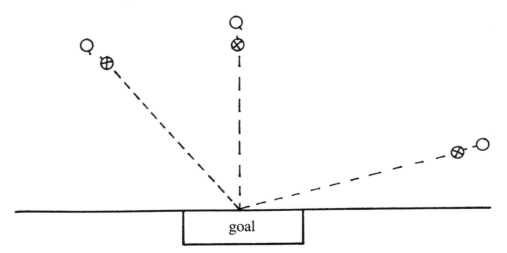

FIGURE 9-6: Marking Distance in Defense

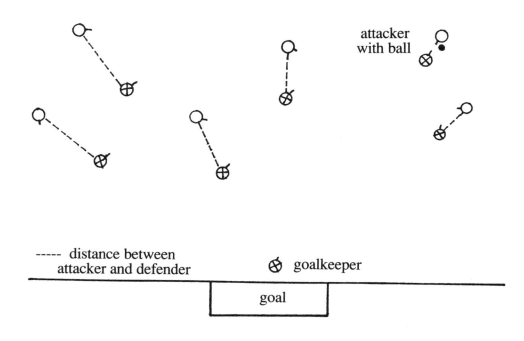

attacker
with ball

----- distance between
attacker and defender

⊗ goalkeeper

goal

When a defender marks the ball carrier, the first priority is to prevent the opponent from turning with the ball and running at you. This is done by *closing down* the attacker as he or she receives the ball (marking goal side from one arm's length). If a defender has to mark an oncoming player already in possession of the ball, he or she should not make a rash and reckless tackle. A tackle should be made only if the ball runs loose or if the defender feels sure of winning the ball. Rather than risk a reckless tackle, it is often necessary to back off from the attacker and keep a distance of about two yards. This is especially important if the rest of the defense needs time to get back in position. This is known as *jockeying* the player with the ball. *Note:* In games in which players are very inexperienced, rash and reckless tackles have a habit of being successful! However, if reckless tackles are made against better dribblers, the flaws in this tactic will be cruelly exposed.

Stance and foot positioning are important factors in sound defending (Figure 9-7). The weight is on the balls of the feet, the center of gravity is low, and the eyes are firmly on the ball. Feet should be positioned *inside* the attacker, blocking the path to the defensive danger zone (Figure 9-8). This forces the attacker to dribble down the sideline and allows the defender to dictate the pattern of play.

FIGURE 9-7: Defensive Stance

FIGURE 9-8: Sidelining the Attacker

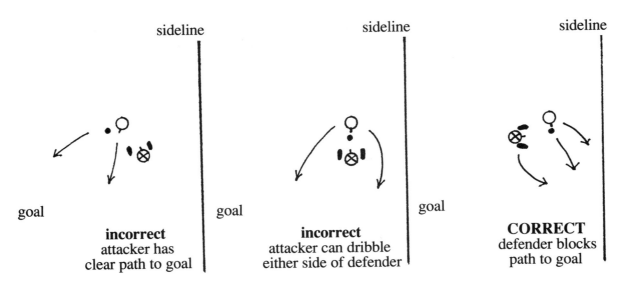

sideline

sideline

sideline

goal

goal

goal

incorrect
attacker has
clear path to goal

incorrect
attacker can dribble
either side of defender

CORRECT
defender blocks
path to goal

10
THROW-INS, GOAL KICKS, CORNERS, AND FREE KICKS

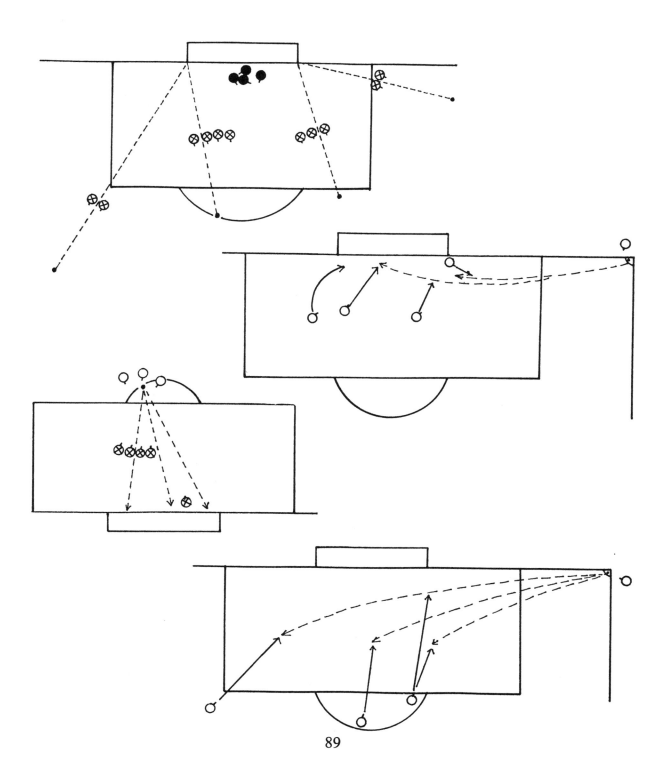

Throw-ins, goal kicks, corners, and free kicks are known as "set pieces." All occur when the ball goes out of play temporarily or when the referee has stopped the game because of an infringement of the laws. Teach players that these are times when quick thinking will often catch a team unprepared, especially in attacking situations. In defense, it is essential that players continue to concentrate when the ball goes out of play or when the referee blows the whistle. Tell players, **"When the ball is dead, we are alive!"**

When the ball goes over the sidelines, the team that last touched the ball will concede a throw-in to the opponent. First, teach your players (and their parents) what constitutes "out of play" (Figure 10-1). The player must use *two* hands to throw the ball in and it must be released *above* the head. Both feet must be in contact with the ground at the point of release and should be on or behind the sideline. A "foul throw" will be awarded by the referee if any of these laws are broken and the throw-in will revert to the other side. It is good policy to strictly referee throw-ins in practice games.

FIGURE 10-1: Ball In and Out of Play

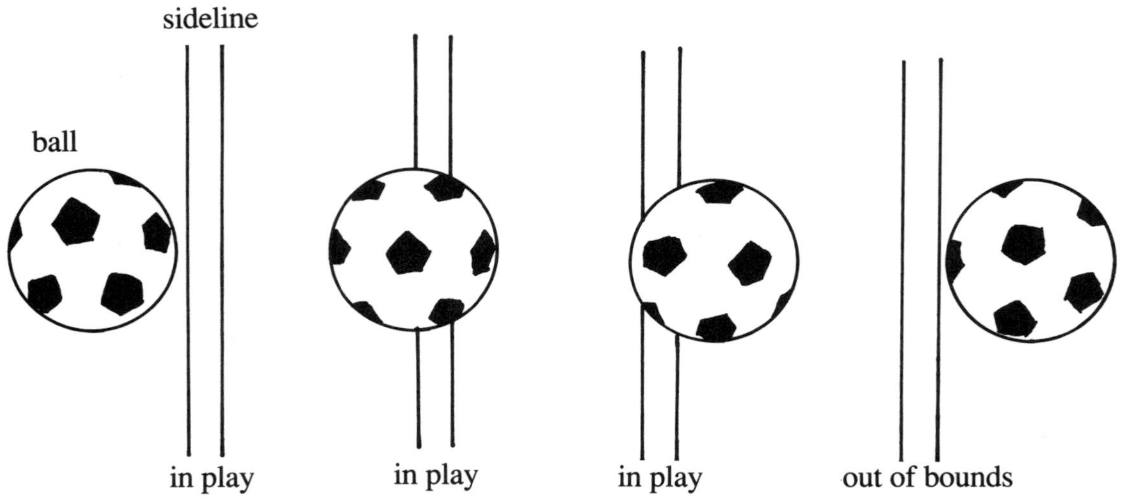

sideline

ball

in play   in play   in play   out of bounds

When taking a throw-in, the feet may be together (Figure 10-2) or split (Figure 10-3). To achieve greater distance, the back should be arched and the arms should be whipped through at great speed. This skill can be easily practiced by pairs of players throwing to each other across a grid. Once players become reasonably competent, hold throw-in competitions for distance and for accuracy.

FIGURE 10-2   FIGURE 10-3

TACTICS AT THROW-INS

As mentioned previously, the quick throw-in can often secure your team safe possession of the ball. To encourage this, tell players to get the ball behind the head as soon as they pick it up. To develop quick thinking in attack and concentration in defense, spread all the spare soccer balls along the lengths of both sidelines. Before the practice game begins, tell players that when the ball goes over the sideline they should pick up the nearest ball and use it for the throw-in.

In general, all throw-ins should be directed *up* the sidelines toward the opponent's goal. In youth soccer, it is not advisable to throw the ball back into the defensive area or across your own goal. A throw-in up the sidelines can take various forms (Figure 10-4).

Throw-Ins, Goal Kicks, Corners, and Free Kicks   **91**

FIGURE 10-4: Options at Throw-Ins

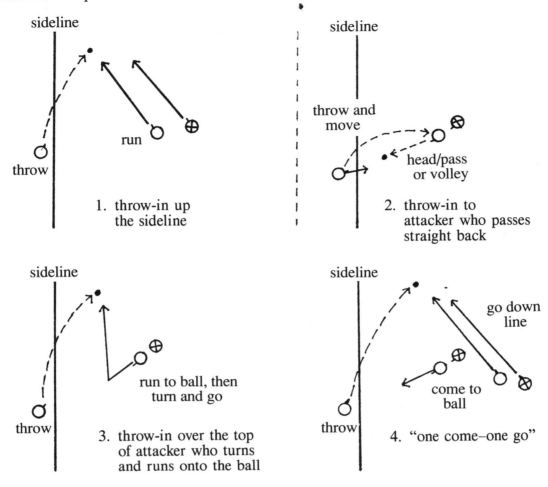

1. throw-in up
   the sideline

2. throw-in to
   attacker who passes
   straight back

3. throw-in over the top
   of attacker who turns
   and runs onto the ball

4. "one come–one go"

GOAL KICKS

If the ball crosses the endline (the goal line) and it was last touched by an attacking player, the referee will award a goal kick. When a player puts the ball back into play from a goal kick, the ball must leave the penalty area before being touched by any other player. Your team should try to keep possession from goal kicks where possible. This may call for a short kick to a defender standing wide. If this option is unsafe, a long clearance kick should be used. Again, direct these kicks down the flanks where there is more space to build an attack.

The goalkeeper *should* take all the goal kicks, with a defender positioned on the edge of the penalty area to guard any lurking attackers and to watch for any miskicks. If the goalkeeper is unable to take the kick, a defender should take it. Never pass the ball *across* the penalty area on a goal kick.

CORNER KICKS

If a defender last touches the ball before it crosses the goal line, the referee will award a corner kick to the attacking side. The kick must be taken from *within* the corner quadrant. The corner flag must not be moved in any way. Corner kicks should be practiced with a flag in position.

Defending at Corner Kicks

There are five main jobs that a team must perform to defend against a corner kick (Figure 10-5):

1. **Pressure the kicker.** By placing a defender the required 10 yards from the ball, the kicker will have an obstacle to kick over and/or around.
2. **Place a defender inside the near post in six-a-side soccer.** Place defenders inside the near and far posts in eleven-a-side soccer. They guard the goal line in case of a shot on goal.
3. **Position the goalkeeper correctly.** For an inswinging corner kick (a kick that arcs toward the goal line) the goalkeeper should be on the goal line. For an outswinging corner kick (a kick that arcs away from the goal line) the goalkeeper should be about two yards off the goal line.
4. **Have all other players mark attackers from about one arm's length away.**
5. **Compete for the ball and clear it away** *long, high,* and *wide.*

FIGURE 10-5: Defensive Positioning at a Corner Kick (Six-a-Side)

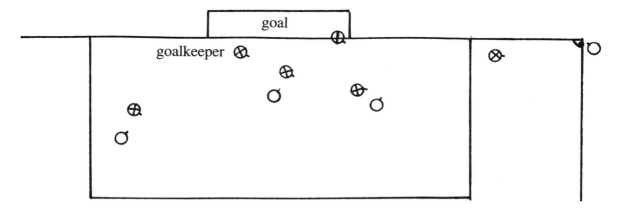

Attacking at Corner Kicks

There are three basic attacking options in a corner kick situation. All have the aim of getting the ball into the defensive danger zone.

1. The *inswinging corner* to the near post or just under the crossbar (Figure 10-6) is an effective option because it tests the goalkeeper's ability to deal with high crosses under pressure. In addition, if the near-post cross can be touched or flicked on, it can often put the goalkeeper and other near-post defenders hopelessly out of position.

FIGURE 10-6: Inswinging Corner—Attacking Positions and Runs on Goal

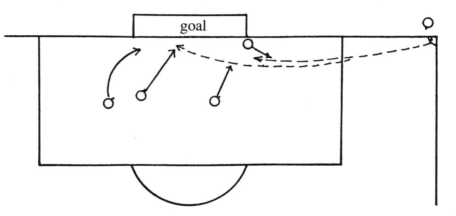

2. The *outswinging corner* should be aimed toward either the penalty spot or the back post (Figure 10-7). It swings the ball away from the goalkeeper and into the path of advancing attackers.

FIGURE 10-7: Outswinging Corner—Attacking Positions and Runs

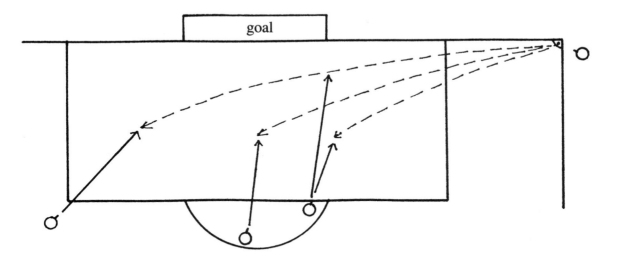

3. The *short corner* (Figure 10-8) often draws defenders away from their marking responsibilities. It also gives the attacking team a better angle from which to swing the ball into or across the goalmouth. There is no point in taking a short corner if the ball is not directed into the goalmouth at some stage.

FIGURE 10-8: Short Corner—Attacking Positions and Runs

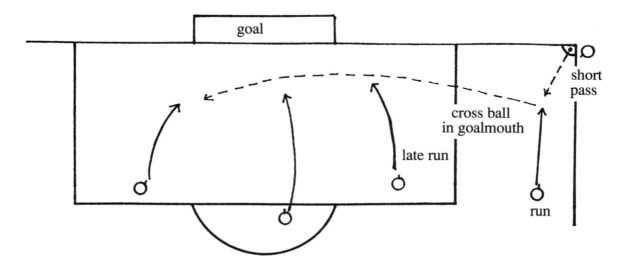

Variations on these three basic themes (such as the low cross to the near post with the attacker suddenly letting the ball through his or her legs) can be made. It is always a good idea to have a player running late to the back post on every single corner. It is amazing how many corner kicks miss everyone and go straight through to the far post!

FREE KICKS

A *direct* free kick is awarded for handball, violent behavior, and other foul play or attempted foul play (for example, tripping, pushing, elbowing, holding, kicking, striking, spitting, and shirt tugging). The ball may be kicked into the goal without having touched another player. An *indirect* free kick is awarded for offsides, obstruction, dangerous play, and other "technical" offenses such as unsportsmanlike conduct or leaving the field without the referee's permission. In this case, the ball must touch at least two different players before crossing the goal line for a score.

Defending at Free Kicks

If a free kick has been awarded away from the defensive danger zone, the team conceding it should follow the normal defensive procedures, that is, running back behind the ball and getting goal side of the player they are marking. If the free kick, direct or indirect, has been awarded within shooting distance of the goal, a *defensive wall* of players should be quickly and accurately constructed. The goalkeeper decides how many players make up the wall and quickly lines them up so the outside player in the wall overlaps a straight line between the ball and the near post. To do this the goalkeeper must stand directly in front of the near post and shout loudly, "Left," "Right," and "Stop," to move the wall to the correct position. The goalkeeper must then run back to cover the area in front of the goal *not* covered by the wall.

Defending against free kicks sounds complicated but becomes easy with practice. The number of players required in the wall increases with the degree of centrality and the closeness of the free kick. Figures 10-9 and 10-10 show the number of players in the wall for both six-a-side and eleven-a-side soccer.

FIGURE 10-9: Positions of Defensive Wall and Goalkeeper at Free Kicks

(Six-a-Side Soccer)

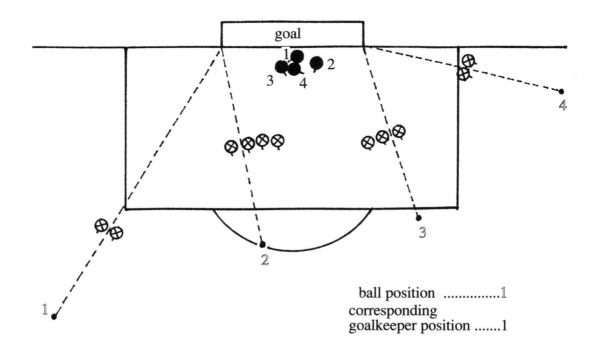

ball position 1
corresponding
goalkeeper position 1

FIGURE 10-10: Positions of Defensive Wall and Goalkeeper at Free Kicks
(Eleven-a-Side Soccer)

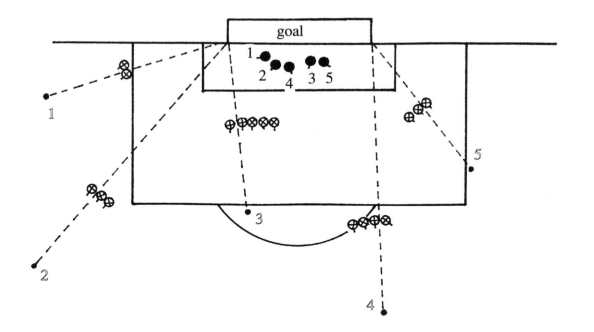

Attacking at Free Kicks

As soon as your side has been awarded a free kick, the nearest player should get to the ball and look up immediately for available options. If a quick kick can set up a good attacking opportunity, take that option. Otherwise, settle on the ball and think it through. When faced with a defensive wall, the attacking side has three main options:

1. Shoot hard at goal, hoping for a gap in the wall or a mistake by the goalkeeper (Figure 10-11). Sometimes a "dummy run" over the ball by an attacker *not* taking the kick can disrupt the defensive wall.

FIGURE 10-11: Shot on Goal by Player A, B, or C

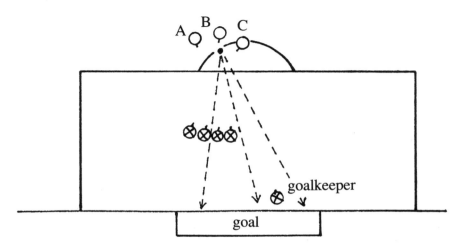

2. Chip or clip the ball over or around the wall to the side of the goal opposite the goalkeeper (Figure 10-12).

FIGURE 10-12: Chip or Clip Over or Around the Defensive Wall

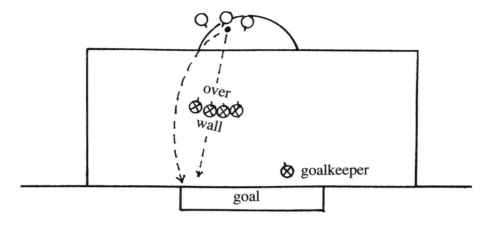

3. Pass or cross the ball to attacking players running in on goal (Figure 10-13).

FIGURE 10-13: Pass or Cross the Ball

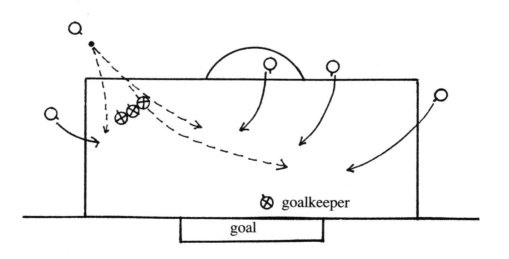

These options should be practiced, but not excessively, as free kicks near the goal are infrequent. Let more experienced players invent free kick options and share the most creative ideas with the rest of the team.

11
GAME DRILLS AND
POSITIONAL PLAY

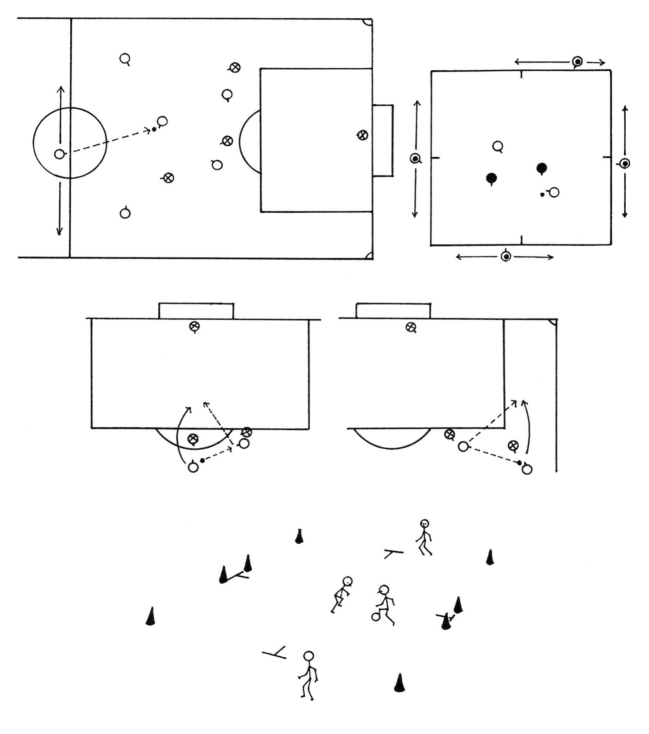

Once a coach has a working knowledge of soccer skills and techniques and has implemented them using the drills in Chapters 4–9, it is time to create game situations in which players can practice their skills. This is best achieved with small-sided games and drills in which participants can be involved as much as possible. The more ball contact players have in a competitive practice situation, the more confident and comfortable they will feel with a ball at their feet during match play.

Small-sided games and drills teach basic *positional play*. They help players learn to:

1. run away from a teammate in possession instead of running to him or her
2. move "off the ball" and create a good passing angle (Figure 11-1)
3. run forward and receive the ball "in space" (Figure 11-2)
4. pass backward to allow the team to move forward

The term positional play also refers to a player's ability to "play a position." As stated previously, players should be taught to play *all* positions, especially when young. In the long run, it is highly ineffective to condition any youngster to play only as a defender or only at any other specific position.

FIGURE 11-1: Creating a Good Passing Angle

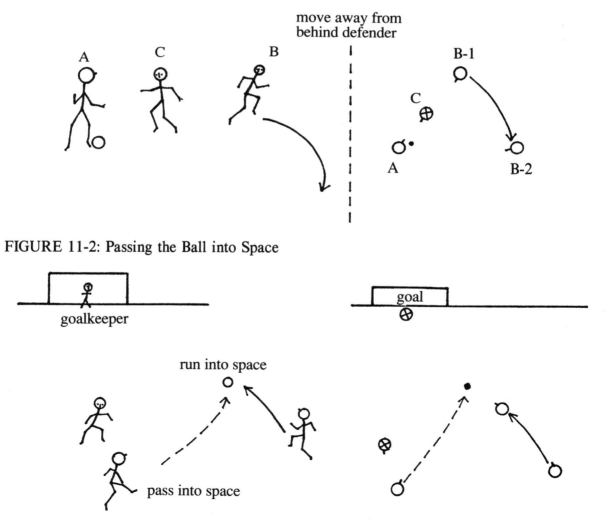

FIGURE 11-2: Passing the Ball into Space

Colored bibs, pinnies, or vests are essential teaching aids for game-type drills. They can be slipped on or held in the hand if quick changes are needed, as in the following drill. This drill is a good starting point for very young players.

GAME DRILL 1 (6 players, 1 ball, 1 4-grid block)

1. For "5 vs. 1," 1 defender stands in the middle of the 4-grid block and the other 5 spread themselves around (Figure 11-3). The player with the ball starts by saying "Go" and then dribbles or passes to teammates. The defender attempts to gain possession of the ball. Change the defender every minute.
   Remind your players:

   • Draw the defender, then pass.
   • Control the ball to the side and keep the head up.
   • Move to create good passing angles.
   • Disguise the pass if possible.

2. Have players try to make 5 passes without an interception. (Increase the number of passes to about 15.)
3. Have players beat the defender with a dribble and then pass to a teammate.

FIGURE 11-3: "5 vs. 1"

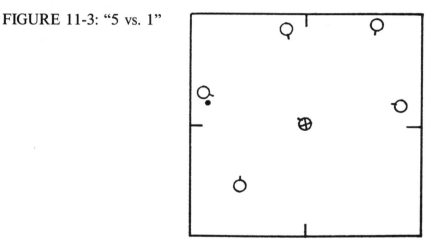

GAME DRILL 2 (5 players, 1 ball, 1 grid)

1. Play "4 vs. 1" with the defender inside the grid and the passers outside the grid (Figure 11-4). Passers try to make as many consecutive passes as possible across the grid without an interception. The 4 on the outside must move to make good passing angles. Change the defender after 1 minute.

FIGURE 11-4: "4 vs. 1"—Passers Outside the Grid

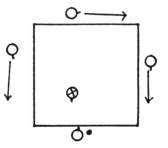

2. Play "4 vs. 1" within a single grid. This places more demands on a player's ball-control and passing skills (Figure 11-5). The outside-of-the-foot pass is a useful technique in this drill.

Remind your players:

- Keep control to the side.
- Use the outside of the foot.
- Use foot, hip, and shoulder fakes.

FIGURE 11-5: "4 vs. 1"—Passers Inside the Grid

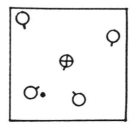

GAME DRILL 3 (5 players, 1 ball, 1 4-grid block)

In "2 vs. 2" with an "assistant," players attempt to score through small goals with the assistant playing for the team that last touched the ball (Figure 11-6). The assistant constantly switches sides, making it a "3 vs. 2" situation. The ball must pass through the goal below the height of the cones. Change the assistant every 2 minutes.

FIGURE 11-6: "2 vs. 2"—with Assistant

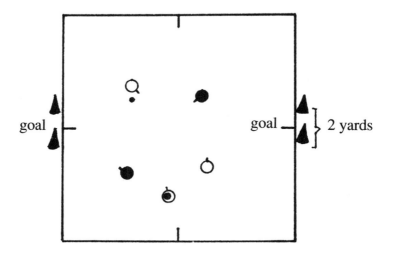

GAME DRILL 4 (4 players, 1 ball, 1 grid)

This is the basic soccer passing drill, "3 vs. 1," because it requires players to "run off the ball" (Figure 11-7). They must move to create a good passing angle with a teammate in possession and learn to pass into space rather than directly to a player.

FIGURE 11-7: "3 vs. 1"

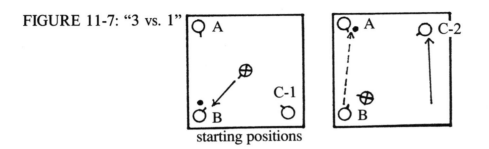

starting positions

GAME DRILL 5 (8 players, 1 ball, 1 4-grid block)

An expanded version of "3 vs. 1," "6 vs. 2" presents the problem of 2 defenders (Figure 11-8). The larger area allows players to switch play from one side to the other and to bisect defenders with a pass. Change defenders every 2 minutes.

Note: If the drill becomes too easy for the passers, change to a "5 vs. 2" situation.

FIGURE 11-8: "6 vs. 2"

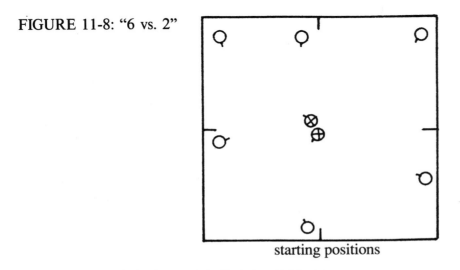

starting positions

GAME DRILL 6 (8 players, 1 ball, 1 4-grid block)

This "2 vs. 2" drill uses no assistant. Because it is more physically demanding, 4 players sit out and 4 players take part. Change teams every 3 minutes (Figure 11-9). The ball must pass through the cones below cone height.

FIGURE 11-9: "2 vs. 2"—No Assistant

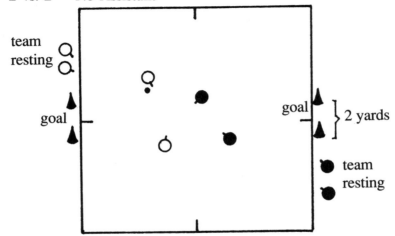

GAME DRILL 7 (6 players, 1 ball, no boundaries)

This "3 vs. 3" drill uses 2 small goals about 30 yards apart (Figure 11-10). There are no boundaries and goals may be scored from in front of or behind the cones. After a goal is scored, the other team starts with the ball in front of its own goal.

FIGURE 11-10:
"3 vs. 3"—No Boundaries

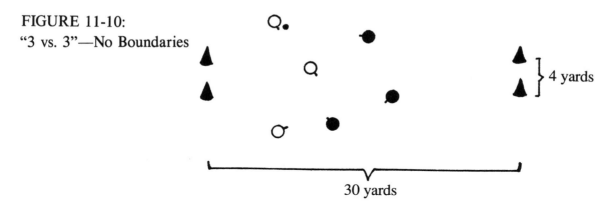

THE "1-2" COMBINATION

The *1-2*, the *wall pass*, and the *give-and-go* all refer to the passing movement in which a player passes the ball to a teammate and then sprints past a defender to receive a quick return pass (Figure 11-11). This combination is slick and effective and can be used to devastating effect in attacking situations (Figure 11-12). Three vital ingredients make up a good 1-2. First, the ball must be played into the "wall" with *pace* and *accuracy*. Second, the original passer must *sprint* into the space behind the defender. And third, the return pass must be directed in *front* of the runner. A wall pass can be executed with any part of the body except the arm and hands.

FIGURE 11-11:
The "1-2" Combination

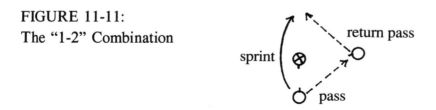

FIGURE 11-12: Using the Wall Pass in Attacking Situations

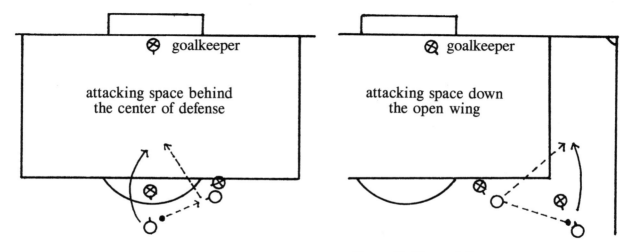

Teach the 1-2 combination only if your players have a reasonably good ability to pass accurately. It is ideally suited to the small-sided drills and games described earlier in this chapter. The following set of drills progressively teaches the wall pass.

GAME DRILL 8 (2 players, 1 ball, 1 grid)

Standing at one end of the grid, player A passes the ball accurately to player B and then sprints forward into space. Player B, with 1 or 2 touches, makes a return pass into the space ahead of A (Figure 11-13). The ball should arrive at the runner's feet without him or her having to check or stutter the stride. Repeat the drill from the opposite side. Switch positions after 3 minutes.

FIGURE 11-13

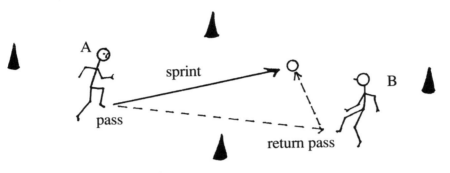

GAME DRILL 9 (2 players, 1 ball, 1 grid)

This drill is exactly the same as Game Drill 8 except player A serves the ball to player B in the air before sprinting for the return (Figure 11-14). Player B then makes a volley, header, or half-volley return into the space ahead of A. Players should be encouraged to experiment with different techniques for moving the ball quickly.

FIGURE 11-14

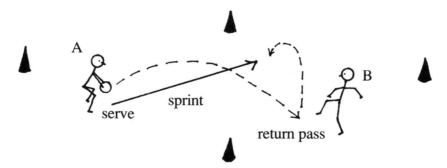

GAME DRILL 10 (3 players, 1 ball, 1 grid)

Add a defender to Game Drills 8 and 9 (Figure 11-15). Have the defender begin in a stationary position so player A can practice passing to one side and running to the opposite side. Gradually have the defender become more active until he or she is operating at full capacity to intercept the ball. Initially, have player A pass the ball in. As players improve have them serve the ball into the wall at varying heights.

Note: If the defender tries to intercept the initial pass, player A should dribble straight through to the other side of the grid.

FIGURE 11-15

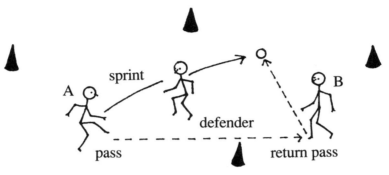

GAME DRILL 11 (4 players, 1 ball, 1 4-grid block)

This is a "1 vs. 1" drill with a small goal at each end of the block. On each side of the block an assistant acts as a wall in a 1-2 movement (Figure 11-16). The assistant plays for whichever side passes the ball in. Each player tries to score into a designated goal, below the height of the cones. After 2 minutes, players and assistants trade places.

FIGURE 11-16: "1 vs. 1"—2 Assistants

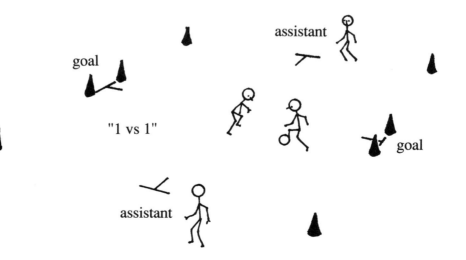

GAME DRILL 12 (8 players, 1 ball, 1 4-grid block)

This is a "2 vs. 2" drill with 4 assistants, 1 on each side of the block (Figure 11-17). Each pair attempts to score as many 1-2 movements as possible in the time allowed. These may be executed with a teammate or an assistant. Where possible, the assistants give a 1-touch return pass. After 3 minutes, players and assistants reverse roles.

FIGURE 11-17: "2 vs. 2"—4 Assistants

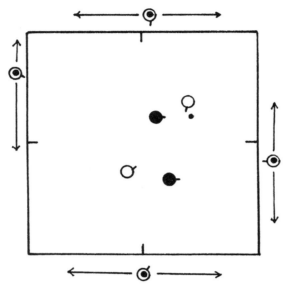

The following drill is actually a pass and move drill that leads into a wall pass drill. (It should not be taught unless players have accurate basic passing skills.) It is an excellent warm-up or pregame exercise and challenges the better players on your team.

GAME DRILL 13 (6–10 players, 1 ball, 1 3-grid channel)

Two lines of 3–5 players face each other across an open grid. Use the following progressions:

1. Player A passes the ball to player B and *jogs* to the end of the opposite line (Figure 11-18).
2. Player A passes the ball to player B and *sprints* to the end of the opposite line.

FIGURE 11-18

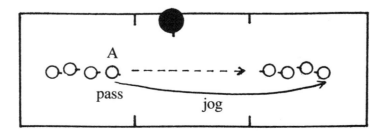

3. Player B moves outward diagonally to the side of the channel to form a wall. Player A th the ball to him or her, sprints onto the return pass from B, and, having controlled it, gives i C, the front player in the opposite line (Figure 11-19). It is essential that player B move out and not forward. Player C then repeats the drill with player D acting as the wall.

FIGURE 11-19

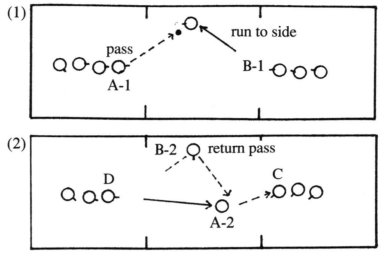

4. Player A picks the ball up and, after player B has moved wide, tosses in a high ball. Player B either volleys or heads a return pass for A to sprint on to. Player C receives the ball and repeats the drill with player D.

5. Introduce a defender who does not try to intercept the ball. The defender stands 2 yards in front of player A (Figure 11-20). As the drill develops, the defender becomes increasingly active. Use ground passes in this drill.

FIGURE 11-20

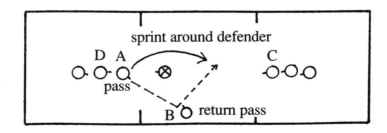

COACHED GAMES

Certain aspects of soccer are best taught and practiced in a game situation. The "coached game" allows the coach to create game situations that bring out specific teaching points. Use a whistle to "freeze" play to make a coaching point, to check on the positioning and balance of the team, or to assess individual positioning.

GAME DRILL 14 (12 players, 1 ball, 1 9-grid block)

This drill is specifically designed to produce crosses into and around the goalmouth. It is a "5 vs. 5" game with a neutral assistant on each flank (Figure 11-21). Assistants play for the team that last touched the ball. Their primary job is to cross the ball into the goalmouth for the attackers to score. The defenders aim to clear and regain possession of the ball. The assistants have a 5-yard wing area in which only they can play. Instruct players how to attack, defend, or keep goal against a variety of cross balls.

FIGURE 11-21

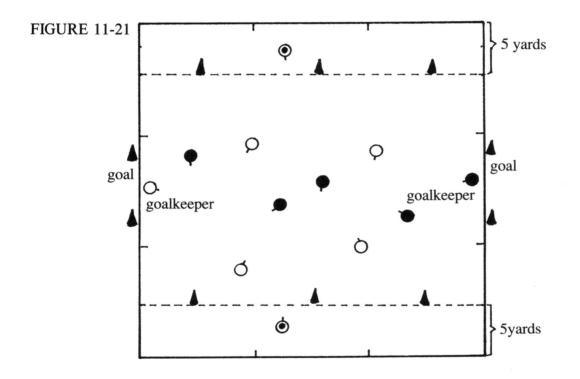

GAME DRILL 15 (whole team, 5 balls, ½ field)

The "half-field coached game" concentrates play into an area that can be easily directed by the coach. A server on the halfway line starts play by passing the ball to a player on the attacking side. Attacking players try to score while defenders try to *accurately* pass the ball back to the server, who may now move anywhere along the halfway line to receive the pass. Goal kicks, throw-ins, corners, and free kicks are awarded as in a regular game. The drill is continuous unless the coach freezes play to make a teaching point. To work on aspects of attacking play, create a "5 vs. 3" situation in favor of the attacking players (Figure 11-22). For eleven-a-side play, an "8 vs. 6" format is more appropriate (Figure 11-23). To improve defensive play, structure a "5 vs. 5" or "8 vs. 8" situation, depending on the number of players. Substitutes can be used freely so all players get a chance to participate and to rest.

FIGURE 11-22: Half-Field Game (Six-a-Side Version)

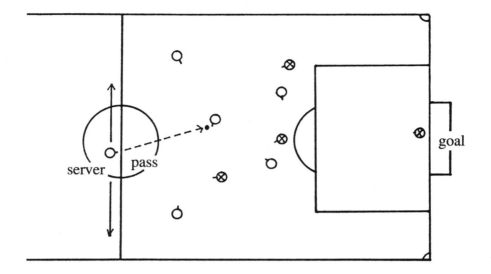

FIGURE 11-23: Half-Field Game (Eleven-a-Side Version)

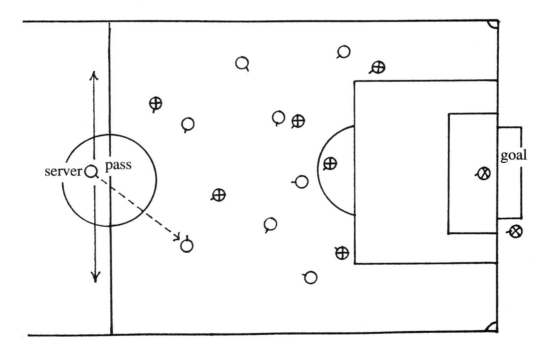

FIGURE 11-24: "6 vs. 6" Practice Game

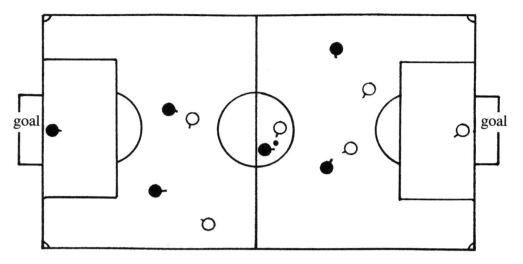

GAME DRILL 16 (whole team, 5 balls, 1 field)

The "6 vs. 6" practice game (Figure 11-24) can be adapted for skilled players in the following ways:

1. Limit the number of touches each player can take (for example, "3-touch" or "2-touch"). Award an indirect free kick for too many touches. This makes players run and work off the ball to produce good passing angles.

2. The player with the ball in the attacking half of the field must beat at least one opponent with a dribble before passing the ball. This encourages players to "take on" their opponents with the ball at their feet.

3. Passes must be below head height. A crisp, low pass is the most efficient method of passing and is a vital technique in windy conditions.

4. Call random free kicks in a dangerous position near goal. This gives both the attack and defense practice in getting organized quickly for free kicks.

5. The team in possession of the ball must move it to within a yard of the sidelines before shooting on goal. This condition encourages players to use the whole width of the field. Often, space on the wings is wasted because players do not go wide (on the sideline). It is much easier to pass the ball directly to a wide player (who can then run at the defense) than to play a through ball or pass to a more central player who is marked (Figure 11-25).

FIGURE 11-25

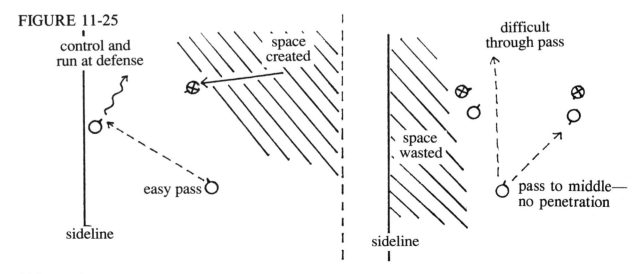

GAME DRILL 17 (8 players, 1 ball, 1 3 × 3 grid area)

"Throw-head-catch" is a game designed to encourage spontaneous heading. Two teams of 4 players compete in the grid area to score a headed goal in one of the two goals (Figure 11-26). The team in possession of the ball must follow the "throw-head-catch" sequence. In other words, if a player throws to a teammate, he *must* head the ball back to any players on the same side. The other team can intercept only on a high ball with a header, not a catch. If the ball goes to the ground the team that last headed it may pick it up. The other team must either head (which is difficult on the ground) or put a knee on it (Figure 11-27) to regain possession. There is no kicking, chesting, etc., in this game.

FIGURE 11-26: Throw-Head-Catch

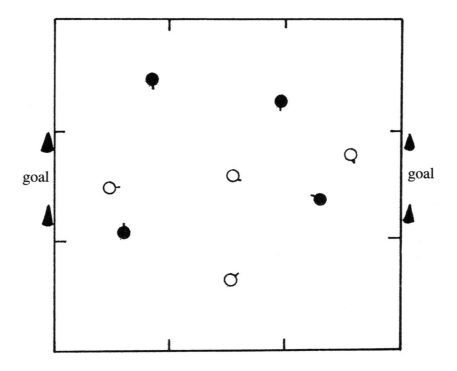

FIGURE 11-27: Reestablishing Possession

knee on ball    reestablishing possession once the ball has gone to ground

GAME DRILL 18 (players 10 and under: 7 players, 1 ball, whole field; players 11 and over: 12 players, 1 ball, whole field)

"Unopposed Soccer" can be used to develop team play and to introduce players to the options open to them when they get the ball into certain areas of the field. The goalkeeper throws or kicks the ball to a teammate; the only initial opposition is the opposing goalkeeper. For players 10 and under, limit the touches to 3; for players 11 and over, limit the touches to 2. Play "6 vs. 1" for players 10 and under, and "11 vs. 1" for players 11 and over. When the ball reaches the other goal, reverse directions and shoot toward the first goalkeeper. Repeat and add defenders when players have mastered the drill.

SOCCER PLAY ACTIVITIES

This section provides activities that youngsters can play on their own. I played many of these when I was a young soccer-playing fanatic in England. They can be played in the park or on the school playground in groups of various sizes. The rules of each game can be easily adapted to suit the group size, skill level, or playing conditions. Kids really do learn a lot of skills, albeit subconsciously, during informal play situations. This is one way of getting kids to practice in their spare time.

Since these are informal games, you may choose to teach them informally. One way of doing this is to play *with* your team at the beginning of the practice session. You can also teach one or two players and then let them teach the others. The games are fun and children enjoy them.

GAME 1 (up to 6 players, 1 ball, 1 goalmouth)

The game called "3 and In" is played with 1 goal and a goalkeeper. The rest of the players go against each other to try to score 3 goals before anyone else. The player that succeeds becomes the goalkeeper. If the goalkeeper saves the ball, he or she kicks it out indiscriminately. If appropriate, use pairs of players instead of singles.

GAME 2 (3–5 players, 1 ball, 1 goalmouth)

"Headers and Volleys" is a simple game in which players try to score 10 goals against the goalkeeper by setting up a series of headers and volleys.

GAME 3 (3–5 players, 1 ball, 1 goalmouth)

The game "29s" is a little more complex than "Headers and Volleys" but it is an excellent way to practice crossing, heading, and goalkeeping. The goalkeeper takes on the rest of the players. Points are awarded *for* various skills and *against* various mistakes. The players try to score 30 points before the goalkeeper scores 29. Players can score only by making goals using the header (5 points). The goalkeeper scores by catching a cross cleanly (2 points), or for mistakes made by the other players: crossing the ball behind the goal is worth 2 points, kicking the ball in goal or handball is worth 3 points.

GAME 4 (up to 5 players, 1 ball, 1 wall)

In "Rebounds" each player must kick the ball against the wall or section of the wall (a 5-yard section is best) in a certain order. Limits may be set on the number of touches each player may use (3, 2, or 1— a first-time kick). If a player misses that section of wall, he or she loses 1 of 3 "lives." The winner is the player that survives with at least 1 "life." Better players might like to try "Volley Rebounds," in which the ball is kicked back after no more than 1 bounce. Players should be encouraged to use both the left and right foot.

GAME 5 (up to 6 players, 1 ball, 1 tennis court or something similar)

"Soccer Tennis" can be played with 1, 2, or 3 players on each side of the net. The idea is to kick the ball into the opponent's court so it bounces more than once. (Beginners should be allowed 2 or 3 bounces.) This usually requires a certain amount of juggling and interplay between players. For a more difficult version, players can head the ball over the net.

GAME 6 (any number of players with 1 ball each)

In "Soccer Golf" players try to take the least number of kicks to hit a variety of targets or "holes." Targets can be trees in the park or cones and obstacles set up by the coach. Players should tackle the "course" with right, left, or alternate feet.

GAME 7 (all players divided into 2 teams, 1 ball, 1 goal, 4 "bases")

"Soccer Baseball" is played like baseball, but the "pitcher" kicks a ground ball to the "batter," who stands in the goal at the midpoint of the goal line. The batter kicks the ball and attempts to run around all the bases before the "fielders," using only their feet, can score into the goal. If the goal is scored before the batter touches home base, the batter is out. If the batter kicks the ball high and a fielder heads the ball on the fly, the batter is out. After 3 outs, players switch places.

There are, without a doubt, many other soccer-related games that you can use in practice sessions. Games keep the players interested and provide a good break from drills.

12
TEAM FORMATIONS

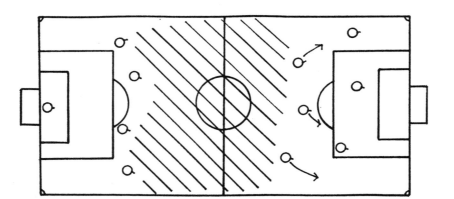

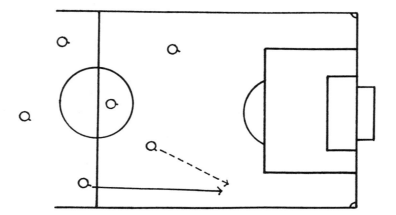

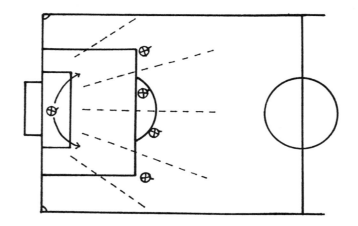

No team formation or system for organizing players can compensate for players without ball skill. As this book is primarily geared to developing skillful young ball players, less emphasis is placed on team systems. Team formations are usually described in terms of the numbers of defenders, midfielders (sometimes called halfbacks), and attackers (also called forwards), in that order. The "2-1-2," "2-2-1," and "1-2-2" formations are used in six-a-side soccer and the "4-3-3," "4-2-4," and "4-4-2" formations in eleven-a-side soccer. The goalkeeper is the sixth (or eleventh) player.

No matter what formation the coach uses, it is important for players to have an understanding of each position. As this understanding grows, the team will begin to function as a single unit, rather than as six or eleven individuals. If a defender is thrusting forward into the attack, a midfield player should have the ability to cover the gap left in the defense. Similarly, if a forward has the ball in a defensive area, he or she should know that greater care should be taken in the distribution of the ball.

SIX-A-SIDE SOCCER

With five "outfield" players, *all* members of the team should be able to shoot, tackle, dribble, and pass the ball effectively. Starting positions depend very much on the strengths of individual players. If you have a strong running midfielder with all-around ability and stamina on your team, a "2-1-2" formation might work (Figure 12-1). In this case, at least one of the two fullbacks must be prepared to push forward and support the attacking effort. The fullbacks can alternate to save energy. The attackers must also be prepared to hustle back and help out in defense if necessary.

The "2-2-1" formation (Figure 12-2) is more defensive and requires players to push forward quickly when in possession to support the lone "front-runner." The forward in this case must have considerable speed and the ability to shield and/or turn on the ball very quickly.

With the "1-2-2" formation, the strongest player is the center back (Figure 12-3). Midfielders must learn to recover quickly toward their own goal if possession is lost. The goalkeeper may also be called upon to rush out and kick the ball away should the center back be beaten.

FIGURE 12-1: "2-1-2" Formation

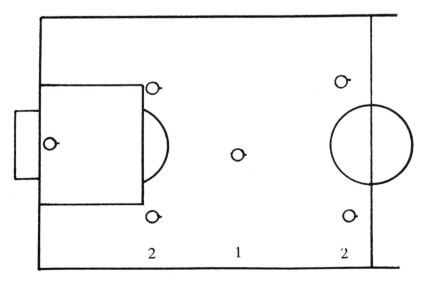

FIGURE 12-2: "2-2-1" Formation

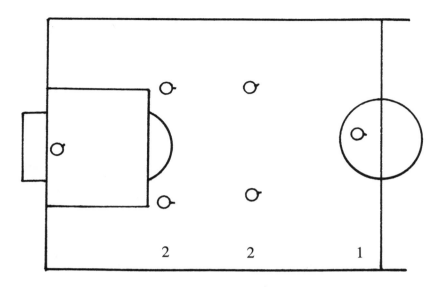

FIGURE 12-3: "1-2-2" Formation

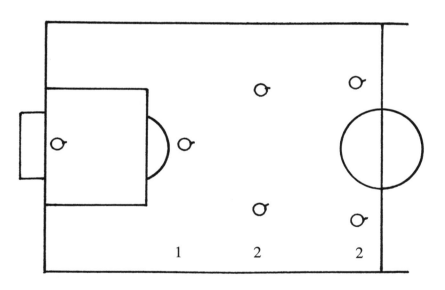

ELEVEN-A-SIDE SOCCER

Most of the back lines in modern soccer utilize four defenders, a fullback on each flank, and two in the center of defense. There is no reason, however, why three defenders cannot be used if the coach thinks they are strong and fast enough. With the four-player back line, central defenders should use either the *zone* or *sweeper* system. In the zone marking system, defenders mark forwards who come into their zone (Figure 12-4). In this system, the golden rule is "leave forwards who run *across* the back four; go with forwards who run *through* the back four."

FIGURE 12-4: Four-Player Back Line Using the "Zone" Marking System

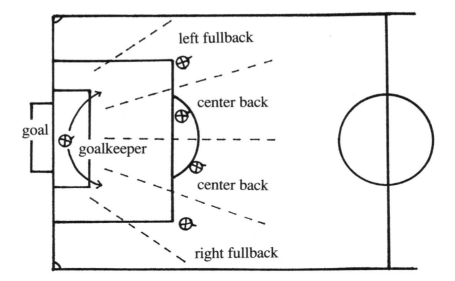

In the sweeper system, three defenders mark the forwards and one player sweeps across the back of the defense to cover for the fullbacks and center back (Figure 12-5). The sweeper should be a player who is fast, skilled, and determined. Because the position does not involve specific marking responsibilities, the sweeper is often free to join in the midfield and the attack.

FIGURE 12-5: Four-Player Back Line Using the "Sweeper" Marking System

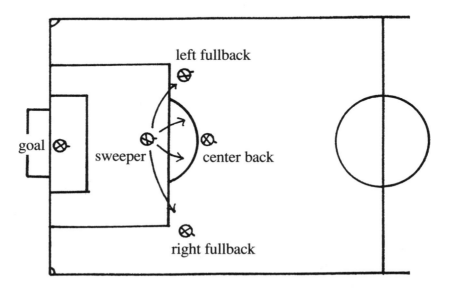

Whether using two or three midfielders, it is vital to have halfbacks who can run with the ball, turn on the ball, pass accurately, and defend stoutly. I always give the following advice to midfielders when they get the ball:

- If you *are* marked, play the ball back to a supporting defender or, preferably, play a quick pass up to your forwards and then run to support that pass.
- If you are *not* marked and there is space ahead of you, run into that space with the ball! Running at the defense with the ball is the best way to pull defenders out of position.

If only two midfielders are used, the fullbacks should be encouraged to "push up" and support the attack from the flank position. The "overlapping fullback" can often act as an extra-wide forward by running into the space down the wings (Figure 12-6).

FIGURE 12-6: The Overlapping Fullback

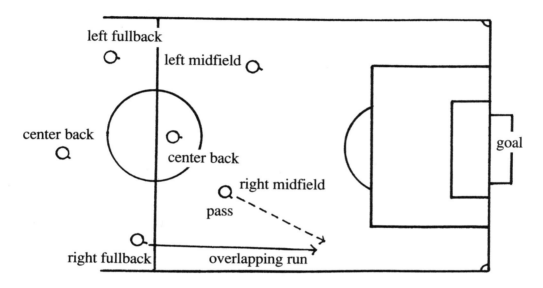

To find the right combination "up front" (that is, on the forward line), the coach must make the best use of the players' abilities. If the forwards are fast, strong, and mobile, three interchanging attackers should be used with three halfbacks to make sure the forwards get a lot of balls passed up to them.

Alternatively, the coach can assign attackers to specific roles such as center forward, inside forward, or winger (Figure 12-7). The center forward is really a "target player" who pushes up into the defensive danger zone to score goals and "lay the ball off" for other players to score. He or she must win the ball when it is played into and around the goalmouth. The inside forward feeds off the balls that are knocked down or flicked on by the center forward. In addition, the inside forward should make frequent diagonal runs into the spaces behind the defensive line.

The winger plays the ball through to the inside forward. The position is so called because it occupies the field area along the sidelines. A winger's first job is to get into position to receive the ball, which often means coming back into the midfield zone. Once in possession of the ball, the winger has three main options:

1. Run at the defense and try to beat the fullback.
2. Cross the ball into the goalmouth for the center forward to contest.
3. Pass the ball into the space behind the defensive line for either the center or inside forwards to chase.

FIGURE 12-7: Forward Positions with Examples of Typical Runs

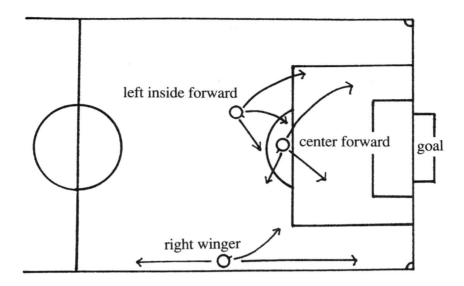

Even though each line of players has been described separately, together they make up a single team unit that must work for a single team effort. If part of the team moves forward the *whole* team—not just the midfield and attack—should move up. If the defense does not move up with the rest of the team or moves up too slowly, play will not be contained within the opponent's half of the field. The gap left between the defense and midfield can be exploited by the opponent if possession is lost or if the ball is cleared away (Figure 12-8).

FIGURE 12-8: Dangers of Defense Not Pushing Up

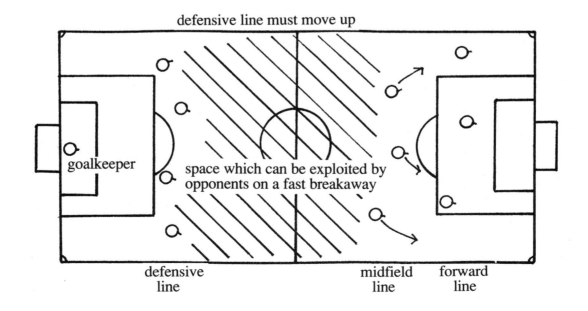

13
SUMMING UP

A great deal of information on skills and drills has been presented in a fairly condensed form in this book. **Be patient in passing on this information**; do not attempt to teach it all in the first three weeks! With younger age groups, select only the very basic skills and drills; it may take two or three seasons before you progress to the more difficult exercises. The drills should not be used only once—they should be repeated at regular intervals until the skill or concept has been truly learned. (A skill can be considered learned if the player can perform it instinctively.) Then introduce more advanced skills and concepts.

As mentioned in Chapter 11, the coach can do only so much in a one-hour practice session. Players must practice and play on their own. This happens naturally in countries where soccer is the national sport. Youngsters watch professional soccer stars on television and their local soccer teams in the park down the road. While they are watching, they are learning. They love to have sports heroes and try to emulate them in their own pick-up games. In the United States, professional soccer has unfortunately not yet found a way to woo the American youngster. You should therefore be especially vigilant in encouraging your players to practice and play on their own time. Unless you can make arrangements for your team to see good quality soccer on a regular basis, however, they will need some other source of motivation and direction.

SOCCER SKILLS AWARDS

One way of developing motivation and direction is to institute a "skills award program." This usually takes the form of a series of soccer skills tests at increasingly difficult levels. Participants receive a certificate and/or badge for passing different stages in the award scheme. This type of motivational tool quickly captures the imaginations of young players and gets them practicing skills like crazy.

A skills award program should be designed so that the lowest level is easy enough for even a rank beginner to pass, with some practice. The highest level should be difficult enough so that even the best young players will have to work hard. Remember that such schemes are not designed to foster competition, although this may occur. Giving skills awards should be utilized as a means to an end, not as an end in itself. The true purpose is to develop skilled soccer players.

THE DAY OF THE GAME

On the day of the big match, meet with the team about 45 minutes before kickoff time. As the players arrive, put them into twos or threes for relaxed passing. When they are all assembled conduct a 15-minute team warm-up that includes jogging and stretching. Then have the forwards take shots on the goalkeepers and have the rest of the team do some simple passing and/or dribbling skills for about 10 minutes. Seven or eight minutes before the start, have a team talk. This should include any final instructions on the way you want them to play as well as some general pointers, such as "Play hard but fair" or "Always play on until you hear the whistle." Finally, tell them to do their best and to enjoy the game.

Those should be your last words until halftime. Soccer is not football or basketball. If the coach has prepared the team well, it will do well. Do not become one of those coaches who constantly shouts instructions from the sidelines. If you do, your players will always wait for your instructions instead of learning to use their own judgment. **Remember that practice time is the coach's time; game time is the players' time. The players are in charge on the field, not the coach.**

A useful coaching aid during games is a simple notepad and pencil. Make notes of positive and negative aspects of your team's play. This will help with your halftime talk and in planning future training sessions.

Be aware of the parents on the sidelines. Make sure that their comments are not detrimental to individual or team efforts. If a parent does make comments you disagree with, deal with that parent as diplomatically as possible. If the parent continues to be insensitive to your wishes, ask him or her not to attend the games.

At the end of the game, have your team shake hands with the opposing team. It is your responsibility as coach to thank both the referee and the opposition's coach.

THE END OF THE SEASON

Many teams like to organize an end-of-season function such as a picnic or barbecue. These are a lot of fun, great for team spirit, and very useful for getting better acquainted with parents and friends. Do not organize a parents versus kids soccer game—someone (usually one of the parents) will get hurt. Instead organize a variety of relay races for parents and kids.

This kind of function is an ideal opportunity to thank those people such as the match secretary, the organizer of treats, the club linesman, etc., who helped off the field. It can also be the time to give skills awards and club awards, if appropriate. Try not to glorify the best players on the team by giving out MVP awards. Present awards for "Most Improved Player," "Best Hustler in Practice," "Best Dribbler," "Best Shooter," and perhaps give a sportsmanship award.

Never forget that you are coaching soccer for the players. However, if you can enjoy the experience too, your players will know it and will help you hang in there for the whole season. Use this book to the fullest—don't keep it on the shelf. Finally, in the words of Crosby, Stills, Nash & Young, "Teach your children well."

APPENDIX I: BASIC LAWS OF SOCCER

Soccer is a team ball game played on a rectangular field with a goal at each end. Each team is comprised of six players (for the youth level) or eleven players. Substitutes can be used, if agreed on by the competing teams or as allowed by the league organizers. The object of the game is to kick, head, or propel the ball by any means (other than with the hand or arm) into the opponent's goal (that is, across the goal line between the two uprights).

Out-of-bounds: If the ball goes completely over the sidelines, whether on the ground or in the air, the team that last touched that ball concedes a throw-in. A player on the opposing team throws the ball in with two hands, releasing it above the head. If the ball goes completely over the end line, either a goal kick (if the ball was last touched by an attacking player) or a corner kick (if it was last touched by a defending player) is made.

Free kicks: A *direct* free kick (a kick that can go directly into the opponent's goal without having to be touched by another player) is awarded for the following law infringements: deliberate handball, pushing, kicking, striking, holding, or tripping an opponent (or attempting to do any of these). An *indirect* free kick (a kick that must be touched by more than one player before a goal can be scored) is awarded for these offenses: obstruction (running in the path of an opponent), dangerous play, offside (see below), other technical offenses such as unsportsman-like conduct, entering or leaving the field of play without the referee's permission, and dissent. With either type of free kick, the ball must be placed at the point of the infringement and it must be stationary. All opponents must be at least 10 yards away from the ball until the free kick has been taken.

Offside: In the eleven-a-side game, the offside law is designed to stop forwards from "goal lurking." The law states that there must be at least two opponents closer to their own goal line than an attacking player when the ball is passed to him/her. In other words, to receive a pass, the player must have the goalkeeper and one other defender closer to the goal line than himself/herself. The ball must be kicked forward for an offside decision, and the player must be in the attacking half of the field.

Goalkeeper: Each team selects a goalkeeper who wears a colored jersey that distinguishes him or her from other players. The goalkeeper is the only player on each team who is eligible to use the hands and arms, and then only in the defending penalty area. Once out of his or her own penalty area, the goalkeeper must abide by the same laws as the rest of the team. Once in possession of the ball (with the ball in the hands), the goalkeeper can take a maximum of four steps before clearing it.

APPENDIX II:
SUCCESSFUL SOCCER

The following model breaks soccer down into four distinct areas, each of which contains a checklist of important skills and concepts. This will simplify the task of analyzing team play, technical strengths and weaknesses, and mental readiness.

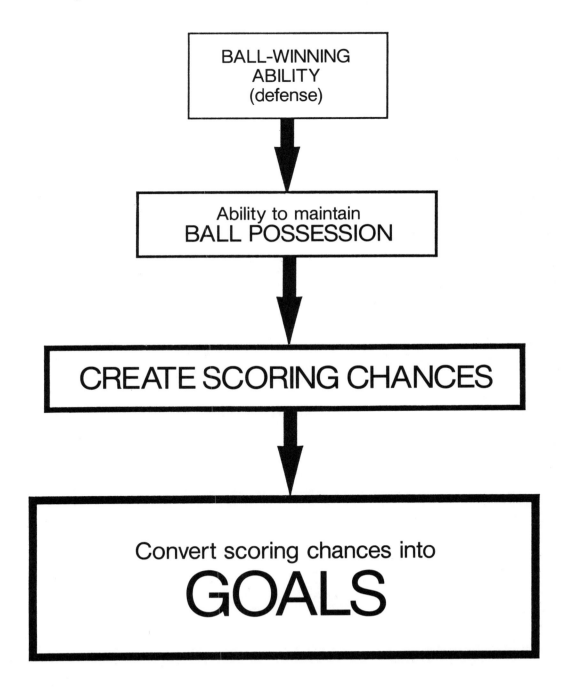

A team can't do anything without the ball!

BALL-WINNING ABILITY
(DEFENSE)

ATTITUDE
- Aggression
- Desire
- Determination
- Composure

FITNESS
- Stamina
- Strength
- Speed
- Agility

TECHNIQUE
- Positioning
- Tackling
   block tackle
   sliding tackle
- Heading
- Stance

TEAM DEFENSE
- Communication
- Balance
- Covering
- Pressuring defense
- Concentration
- Organization at set pieces

SOUND GOALKEEPING
- Correct technique
- Correct practice
- Confidence
- Leadership

Once the ball is won, it must be advanced toward the opponent's goal.

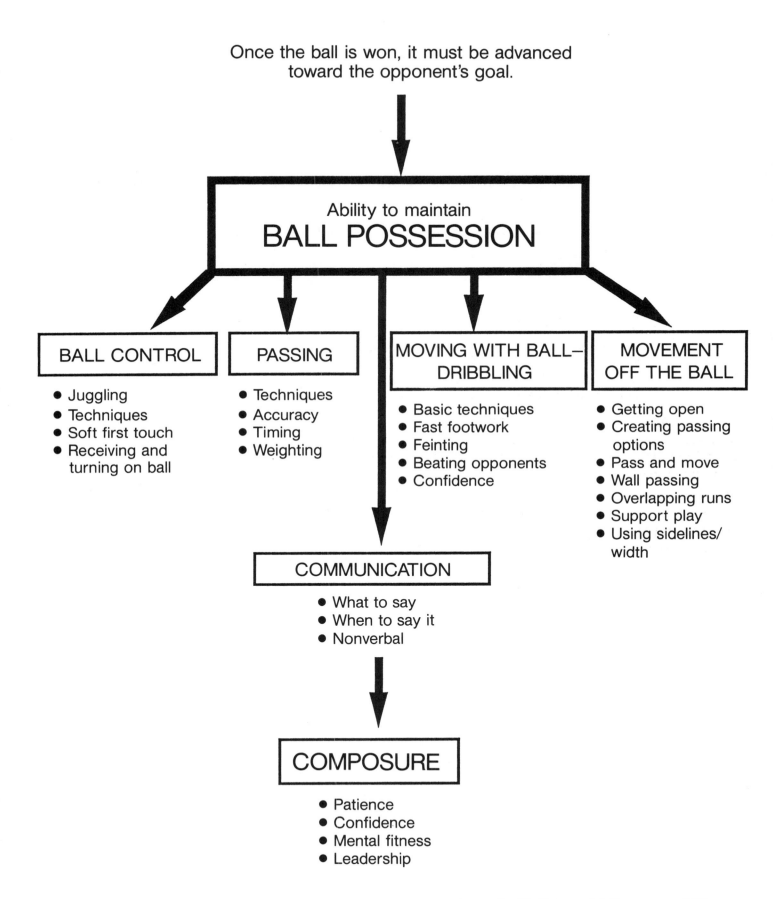

Ability to maintain
BALL POSSESSION

BALL CONTROL
- Juggling
- Techniques
- Soft first touch
- Receiving and turning on ball

PASSING
- Techniques
- Accuracy
- Timing
- Weighting

MOVING WITH BALL— DRIBBLING
- Basic techniques
- Fast footwork
- Feinting
- Beating opponents
- Confidence

MOVEMENT OFF THE BALL
- Getting open
- Creating passing options
- Pass and move
- Wall passing
- Overlapping runs
- Support play
- Using sidelines/ width

COMMUNICATION
- What to say
- When to say it
- Nonverbal

COMPOSURE
- Patience
- Confidence
- Mental fitness
- Leadership

Once near the opponent's goal, a team must

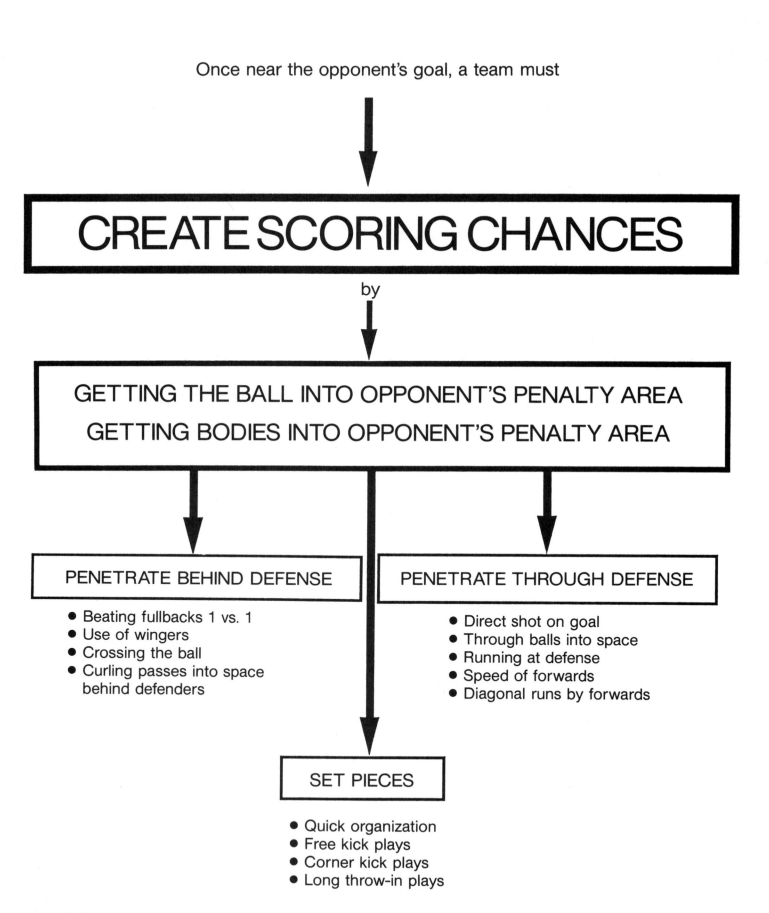

CREATE SCORING CHANCES

by

GETTING THE BALL INTO OPPONENT'S PENALTY AREA

GETTING BODIES INTO OPPONENT'S PENALTY AREA

PENETRATE BEHIND DEFENSE

- Beating fullbacks 1 vs. 1
- Use of wingers
- Crossing the ball
- Curling passes into space behind defenders

PENETRATE THROUGH DEFENSE

- Direct shot on goal
- Through balls into space
- Running at defense
- Speed of forwards
- Diagonal runs by forwards

SET PIECES

- Quick organization
- Free kick plays
- Corner kick plays
- Long throw-in plays

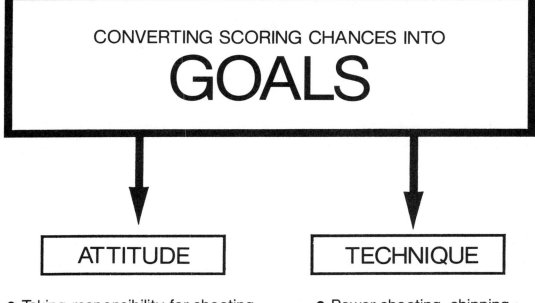

CONVERTING SCORING CHANCES INTO
GOALS

ATTITUDE

- Taking responsibility for shooting and sometimes missing
- Think shoot, shoot, shoot!
- Following shots, expecting rebounds
- Bravery
- Opportunism
- Composure

TECHNIQUE

- Power shooting, chipping
- Improvisation
- Heading for goal
- Volleying for goal
- Converting breakaways
- Far-post shots
- Clinical finishing—repetition

APPENDIX III:
TEN-WEEK SEASON PLANS

SEASON PLAN FOR AGES 7–10
Ten-Week Plan—Two Practice Sessions per Week
Recommended Length of Practice Sessions: Ages 7–8, 50 Minutes
Ages 9–10, 60 Minutes

WEEK 1
1. Dribbling warm-up/stretching
   Teach simple juggling techniques
   Teach basic passing and control
   5 vs. 1 in a 20 × 20, 4 consecutive passes
   3 vs. 3 mini soccer games, small goals
2. Dribbling warm-up/stretching
   Review juggling, set targets
   Review passing and control
   5 vs. 1 in a 20 × 20, 6 consecutive passes
   3 vs. 3 mini soccer games, small goals

WEEK 2
1. Warm-up/stretching/juggling
   Dribbling Drill 1/"King of the Circle"
   Teach basic chest control/thigh control
   3 vs. 3 mini soccer, small goals
2. Warm-up/stretching/juggling
   Repeat Dribbling Drill 1/"King of the Circle"
   5 vs. 1, then 4 vs. 1 in grids
   3 vs. 3 mini soccer, small goals

WEEK 3
1. Warm-up/follow the leader with ball
   Pass/Control Drill 8, move to ball
   Teach basic heading, up and down
   3 vs. 3 mini soccer
2. Warm-up/juggling/stretching
   Review heading, pass and move in triangles
   Teach throw-ins and combine with ball control
   3 vs. 3 with throw-ins

WEEK 4
1. Warm-up/stretching/cone dribbling
   Heading in pairs, review throw-ins
   Teach basic goalkeeping to whole team
   4 vs. 4 play, rotate goalkeepers
2. Stretching/4 vs. 1 warm-up
   Teach shooting technique
   Shooting Drill 3, review goalkeeping
   4 vs. 4 play, rotate goalkeepers

WEEK 5
1. Stretching/juggling warm-up
   Review shooting technique
   Teach move to beat opponent, outside-of-foot
   Dribbling Drill 5/4 vs. 4 play
2. Stretching/juggling
   Teach fake and cut back/Dribbling Drill 4
   Explain positions in 6 vs. 6
   Play 6 vs. 1 "Unopposed Soccer"

WEEK 6
1. Stretching/dribbling drill with cones
   Teach "block tackle," defensive stance
   Play 1 vs. 1, emphasize stay on feet
   6 vs. 1 "Unopposed Soccer," then 6 vs. 6
2. Stretching/pass and move drill
   Review and practice block tackle and 1 vs. 1
   Teach "Throw-Head-Catch" game, 4 vs. 4
   6 vs. 6 play

WEEK 7
1. Stretching/Dribbling Drill 1
Teach shooting for far post
Practice corner kicks, free kicks
6 vs. 2 "Unopposed Soccer"/6 vs. 6 play
2. Stretching/dribbling/juggling
Emphasize shooting quickly and often
Shooting Drill 5, improvised shooting
6 vs. 6 play—lots of shots on goal!

WEEK 8
1. Stretching/juggling
Introduce 3 vs. 1 in a grid
Teach and practice jumping headers
"Throw-Head-Catch," then 6 vs. 6 play
2. Stretching/3 vs. 1 warm-up
Heading for goal, Heading Drill 7
Teach 1-touch passing
6 vs. 6 conditioned game, coach width

WEEK 9
1. Stretching/3 vs. 1 2-touch
6 vs. 2 Keepaway, 1 point for splitting defenders
Crossing, Game Drill 14
6 vs. 6 conditioned game 9, 3-touch, then 2-touch
2. Stretching/1-touch passing
5 vs. 2 in a grid, 4 consecutive passes
Practice long passing, then Shooting Drill 4
Half-field game, 6 vs. 4

WEEK 10
1. Stretching/5 vs. 2 possessions drill
Improvised Shooting Drill 3
"Throw-Head-Catch"
6 vs. 6 game, coach diagonal runs by forwards
2. Stretching/juggling/1-touch passing
2 vs. 2 play, Pressuring and Covering
Attacking and defending at free kicks
6 vs. 6 play—3-touch, then 2-touch

SEASON PLAN FOR AGES 11–14

Ten-Week Plan—Two Practice Sessions per Week

Recommended Length of Practice Sessions: Ages 11–12, 80 Minutes
Ages 13–14, 100 Minutes

WEEK 1
1. Warm-up/juggling/dribbling skills
Passing/ball control over 10 yards
4 vs. 1 game drill in a grid
3 vs. 3 play, small goals
2. Warm-up/juggling/dribbling skills
Chest/thigh control, basic heading
4 vs. 1 game drill in a grid
3 vs. 3 play, small goals

WEEK 2
1. Warm-up/juggling/cone dribbling
Passing/control over 15–20 yards
Jumping headers, tackling technique
4 vs. 4 play, goals, rotate goalies
2. Warm-up/juggling/beating opponents
1-touch passing, trapping high balls
3 vs. 1 Keepaway in grids
4 vs. 4 play—rotate goalies

WEEK 3
1. Warm-up/juggling/ball control skills
Shooting technique—Shooting Drills 1 and 2
Shooting Drill 3
"Throw-Head-Catch"
2. Warm-up/juggling/dribbling skills
Pass/control over 20 yards, chipping
3 vs. 1 Keepaway, Shooting Drill 4
6 vs. 6 play, coach movement off the ball

WEEK 4
1. Warm-up/juggling/beating opponents
Beating defenders, Dribbling Drill 4
Wall passes, Game Drill 8
6 vs. 8 half-field game (8 attackers)
2. Warm-up/juggling/practice fakes
Improvised shooting drill in penalty area
1 vs. 1 with assistants, Game Drill 12
8 vs. 6 half-field game (8 defenders)

WEEK 5
1. Warm-up/juggling/ball-control skills
   1-touch passing/lofted drives
   Pass and move, Game Drill 13
   6 vs. 6 conditioned game, coach width
2. Warm-up/juggling/dribbling skills
   Volleying techniques/volleying for goal
   Crossing, Game Drill 14
   6 vs. 6 conditioned game, 2-touch

WEEK 6
1. Warm-up/juggling/dribbling skills
   Individual defense, pressuring/covering
   6 vs. 2 Keepaway in a 40 × 40 grid
   6 vs. 6 play, coach pressure defense
2. Warm up/juggling/practice fakes
   Defensive heading/receiving and turning
   6 vs. 2, then 5 vs. 2, then 2-touch
   6 vs. 6 play, coach quick shooting

WEEK 7
1. Warm-up/dribbling with passive defense
   Wall pass drill, Game Drill 13
   Throw-ins, techniques, and set plays
   Two games of 4 vs. 4 or 3 vs. 3
2. Warm-up/team juggling/dribbling skills
   Far-post shooting, follow up for rebounds
   1-on-1 dribbling vs. goalkeeper
   7 vs. 7, coach quick shooting

WEEK 8
1. Warm-up/juggling/beating opponents
   Wing play and crossing as a skill
   Review attacking heading/volleying
   Repeat crossing, Game Drill 14
2. Warm-up/head juggling in pairs
   Free kicks on defense, setting up a wall
   Free kicks on offense, beating the wall
   7 vs. 7 with referee calling many fouls near goal

WEEK 9
1. Warm-up/juggling/control skills
   5 vs. 2, coach quick, accurate passing
   Corner kick plays, learn 3 good ones
   "Unopposed Soccer," 11 vs. 1 (the goalie)
2. Warm-up/juggling/dribble and shoot
   3 vs. 1 Keepaway, 2-touch, then 1-touch
   7 vs. 7, coach diagonal runs by forwards
   7 vs. 6 in favor of attackers, half-field game

WEEK 10
1. Warm-up/juggling/juggle and shoot
   Passing over 40 yards, passive defense
   "Throw-Head-Catch," teach diving header
   7 vs. 7 playing time, coach "relax on ball"
2. Warm-up/juggling/juggle and shoot
   Improvised shooting drill
   Review pressure defense and covering
   7 vs. 7, quick transition from defense to midfield

SEASON PLAN FOR AGES 15–19
Ten-Week Plan—Two Practice Sessions per Week
Recommended Length of Practice Sessions: 120 minutes

WEEK 1
1. Warm-up/stretching/juggling
   Passing over 10, 20, 30 yards/dribbling
   3 vs. 1 in grids, coach outside-of-foot pass
   3 vs. 3 games, small goals
2. Warm-up/stretching/juggling
   1-touch passing/dribbling technique
   3 vs. 1, coach fakes, then 6 vs. 2, big grid
   3 vs. 3 games, small goals

WEEK 2
1. Warm-up/stretching/pairs juggling
   Practice chipping ball over defender in 3s
   3 vs. 1, coach back heels, then 6 vs. 2
   3 vs. 3, no boundaries, Game Drill 7
2. Warm-up/stretching/head juggling
   Chipping ball, swerving, inside/outside
   3 vs. 1, coach 2-touch, use complete grid
   4 vs. 4 games, rotate goalkeepers

WEEK 3

1. Stretching/pairs juggling, 4 exchanges
   Low drives, 40 yards/dribbling technique
   5 vs. 2 Keepaway, then 2-touch
   6 vs. 6 play, coach width in attack
2. Stretching/head juggling between pairs
   Lofted drive/dribbling technique
   5 vs. 2, coach takeovers
   6 vs. 6 play, coach diagonal runs

WEEK 4

1. Stretching/juggling, 25 minimum
   Moves to beat opponents
   Individual defensive stance, principles, 1 vs. 1
   6 vs. 6 play, coach defense
2. Stretching/double head juggling between pairs
   Moves to beat opponents
   Defense, pressuring/covering, 2 vs. 2
   6 vs. 6 play, coach width in attack

WEEK 5

1. Stretching/figure-8 heading in 4s
   Tackling technique/dribbling technique
   Wall passing in pairs, Game Drill 13
   8 vs. 8, coach movement, communication
2. Stretching/figure-8 heading in 4s
   Moves to beat opponents, passive defense
   Shooting technique, Shooting Drills 1, 2, 3
   8 vs. 8 play, coach shooting attitude

WEEK 6

1. Warm-up/stretching/pairs juggling
   1-touch passing, Game Drill 13
   The far-post shot, Shooting Drill 4
   "Throw-Head-Catch," then 8 vs. 8 free play
2. Warm-up/stretching/pairs juggling
   Receiving and turning, Dribbling Drill 6
   Dribble past defender and shoot
   8 vs. 8, throw-in plays

WEEK 7

1. Stretching/juggling—35 minimum
   Volleying technique—laces/side/shoot
   Crossing as a skill, stationary/on run
   Crossing, Game Drill 14, coach offense
2. Stretching/juggling—40 minimum
   Volleying for goal from a toss
   "Throw-Head-Catch"
   Crossing, Game Drill 14, coach defense

WEEK 8

1. Stretching/juggling—across a 20-yard grid
   Backheaders/flick-ons/shielding ball
   Improvised Shooting Drill 5
   8 vs. 6 half-field game
2. Stretching/juggling across a 20-yard grid
   Receiving and turning, active defense
   Free kicks and corners, defensive set-up
   8 vs. 8, call many free kicks near the box

WEEK 9

1. Stretching/juggling/figure-8 heading
   Two games of 4 vs. 4, 2-touch
   Free kicks and corners, offensive plays
   8 vs. 8, call many free kicks near box
2. Stretching/juggling—50 minimum
   2 vs. 2 with assistants, Game Drill 12
   Overlapping runs by fullbacks/midfield
   "Unopposed Soccer," 11 vs. 1, then 11 vs. 4

WEEK 10

1. Stretching/juggling in pairs
   Diving headers, overhead kicks
   Near-post runs/far-post runs
   8 vs. 8 play, coach diagonal runs
2. Stretching/juggling competition
   Turning and shooting, active defense
   1 vs. goalie breakaway, then add defender
   8 vs. 8 play, try 1-touch

- 10 minutes of fitness training should be done at the end of each session.
- Goalkeeper training should be included, using the assistant coach. (Use goalkeepers for all shooting drills.)

GLOSSARY OF SOCCER TERMS

Assistant—Assists the team that last touched the ball (in drills).

Away swing—A kick that swerves the ball away from the goal.

Back header—Glancing or flicking the ball behind with the head.

Ball familiarization—The practice of making children comfortable with a soccer ball by using it in familiar situations such as stretching.

Block—A large square practice area made up of at least four grids.

Block tackle—A foot tackle onto the ball from a standing position.

Center forward—An attacking player who operates primarily in the middle of the forward line.

Channel—Two or more grids joined together end to end.

Chip pass—A lofted or high pass, often with backspin.

Closing down (an attacker)—When a defender reduces the distance between himself or herself and an attacker with the ball.

Coached game—A practice game in which the coach will often freeze play to make a coaching point.

Conditioned game—A practice game in which the coach imposes restrictions or conditions on the players.

Cross—A pass across the face of the goal.

Dangerous play—A technical offense awarded against a player who endangers other players or himself/herself.

Defensive danger zone—The area in front of goal from which most goals are scored.

Dummy run—A decoy run by a player.

Far post—The goalpost farthest from the ball.

Filling in—Temporarily covering a teammate's position.

Flank—The sides or wing areas of the field.

Forward—An attacking player.

Foul throw—An illegal throw-in.

Front-runner—An attacking player who often waits upfield and acts as a target player.

Goal line—The line between the two goalposts.

Goalmouth—The area just in front of the goal.

Goal side—The position a defender takes up when marking an attacker, that is between the attacker and the defender's own goal.

Half-volley—A kick on the ball as, or just after, it bounces.

Handball—Use of the hand or arm to control the ball by an outfield player.

Inside forward—An attacking player who plays in front of the center forward and often feeds off his or her passes and flicks.

In space—In an area of the field not occupied by other players.

In swing—A kick that swerves the ball in toward the goal.

Jockeying—Retreating with an attacker to buy time for the rest of the defense.

Juggling—Keeping the ball off the ground with the feet, thighs, and head.

Laying the ball off—Passing the ball to a teammate, usually one-touch.

Man on—The call a player makes to a teammate who is closely marked but may not be aware of it.

Marking—Tracking or covering an attacker.

Narrowing the angle—A goalkeeper advancing to present a larger obstacle to the shooter.

Near post—The goalpost nearest the ball.

Obstruction—Blocking an opponent with the body when not in a position to play the ball.

Off the ball—Away from the ball.

One-touch pass—A first-time pass using only one kick

Outfield players—Those who do not play as goalkeeper.

Overlapping fullback—A fullback who runs down the wing area to collect a pass and become an additional attacker.

Passing angle—The angle between the passer and the potential receiver in relation to the pressuring defender. A good passing angle allows a player to pass to a teammate with no defenders in between.

Push up—To run up toward the opponent's end of the field.

Set pieces—Throw-ins, corner kicks, goal kicks, free kicks, and penalties.

Shielding—Guarding the ball from opponents with the body.

Sidelining the attacker—When a defender forces the attacker to dribble to the side of the field.

Skill progressions—A sequence of drills designed to gradually teach players a new skill or technique.

Sliding tackle—When the defender slides in with one foot to kick the ball away from an opponent.

Small-sided drill—Drill that includes only a few players.

Sweeper—A defensive player who covers across and behind the other defenders.

Tackle—To kick the ball away from an opponent with the foot.

Take on—To beat a defender with a dribble.

Target man—An attacking player who acts as a target for forward passes.

Tie-up—Strapping that keeps socks and shinguards in place.

Volley—A kick on the ball while it is in the air.

Wall pass—When the dribbler passes the ball to a teammate (the wall) and runs on to the return pass.

Zone defense—A defensive system in which each player covers a zone and marks players who enter it.

INDEX

Angles
 goalkeeping, 78
 narrowing, 79–80
Assistant, 132
Attackers, 115
Attitude
 importance of, 5
 toward shooting, 59
Away swing, 132

Back header, 56–57, 132
Balance, 17
Ball control, 26
 bringing a ball down on the laces, 32–34
 chest control, 31
 contact areas for, 26–28
 pass/control drills, 29–34
 thigh control, 32
Ball familiarization, 132
Ball handling
 dribbling, 36–46
 goalkeeping, 69–81
 heading, 48–57
 shooting, 59–61
 volleying, 66–68
Ball winning
 drills in, 83
 individual defense, 86–88
 tackling, 84–85
Banana kick, 25
Block, 132
Block tackle, 84, 132

Calisthenics, 21
Center forward, 118, 132
Channel, 132
Chest control, 31
Chip pass, 25, 132
Closing down, 87, 132
Coached games, 108, 132
 "5 vs. 3," 108
 "5 vs. 5," 108
 "6 vs. 6," 110
 "8 vs. 6," 108
 "8 vs. 8," 108
 "half-field coached game," 108–9
Coaching, versus teaching, 5
Conditioned game, 132
Corner kicks, 92
 attacking at, 93–94
 defending at, 92–93
Corners, 90
Crosses, 132
 dealing with, 81
Cruyff, Johan, 36

Dangerous play, 132
Day of the game, 121
Dealing with crosses, 81

Defenders, 115
 beating with dribble, 40–44
Defensive aspects, 85
 individual defense, 86–88
 team defense, 85–86
Defensive danger zone, 132
Defensive wall, 95
Determination, 5
Direct free kick, 122
Distributing the ball, 76–77
Diving, position of readiness for, 73
Dribbling, 36–38
 beating defenders, 40–44
 drills in, 39–40, 42–46
 receiving and turning on the ball, 44–46
 shielding the ball, 46
Dummy run, 96, 132

Eleven-a-side soccer, 13, 116–19
End of the season, 121
Equipment, importance of correct, 9

Fair play, 5
Far post, 132
Filling in, 132
Flank, 132
Foot, juggling with, 16
Footwear, 9
Forward, 115, 132
Foul throw, 90, 132
Free kicks, 90, 95, 122
 attacking at, 96–97
 defending at, 95–96
 direct, 95, 122
 indirect, 95, 122
Front-runner, 132
Fullbacks, 115, 118
Fun, importance of, 5

Game day, 121
Game drills, 99–103
 "1 vs. 1" drill, 105
 "2 vs. 2" drill, 101, 102
 "2 vs. 2" drill, 106
 "3 vs. 1" drill, 101–2
 "3 vs. 3" drill, 103
 "4 vs. 1" drill, 100
 "5 vs. 1" drill, 100
 "6 vs. 2" drill, 102
Give-and-go, 103
Goal, volleying for, 66–68
Goalkeeper, 115, 122
 mental qualities of, 70
 physical qualities of, 70
Goalkeeping, 70
 angles, 78
 collecting the ball, 70–72
 dealing with crosses, 81
 distributing the ball, 76–77

narrowing the angle of shots, 79–80
punching the ball clear, 80–81
shot stopping, 73–75
techniques for, 70–81
Goal kicks, 90, 92
Goal line, 133
Goal side, 133
Goalmouth, 133

Halfbacks, 115
Half-field coached game, 108–9
Half-volley, 64, 133
kicked clearance, 77
Hand position, for catching a high ball, 72
Handball, 133
Head, 16
Head juggling, 16
Head-catch, 50
Headers and volleys, 112
Heading, 48
back header, 56–57
drills in, 49–57
introducing opposition, 55–56
jumping to head the ball, 52–55
teaching, 49–51

Improvised shooting, 63–64
Indirect free kick, 122
Individual defense, 86–88
Inside forward, 118, 133
In space, 133
In swing, 133
Instep drive, 25
Inswinging corner, 93
Inswinging pass, 25

Javelin pass, 76
Jockeying, 87, 133
Juggling, 16–17, 133
drills in, 17–19
teaching, 17–19
with the foot, 16
Jumping to head the ball, 52–55

Kick, faking, 41
Kicking action, 23
King of the circle, 39
Kneeling technique, 70, 71

Laying the ball off, 133

Man on, 133
Maradona, Diego, 36
Marking, 133
Midfielders, 115, 118

Narrowing the angle, 133
Near post, 133
Near-post rebounds, 62

Obstruction, 133
Offside, 122

Off the ball, 133
"1-2" combination, 103–7
1-2-2 formation, 115, 116
One-touch pass, 133
Opposition, introducing, 55–56
Organizational tips, 9–14
Outfield players, 133
Out-of-bounds, 122
Outside-of-the-foot pass, 24
Outswinging corner, 94
Overhand throw, 76
Overlapping fullback, 118, 133

Pace, change in, 37
Parents, role of, at soccer games, 9
Pass/control drills, 29–34
Passing
instep drive, 25
outside-of-the-foot pass, 24
sidefoot pass, 23
Passing angle, 133
Pelé, 6, 36
Pivot turn, 44–45
Positional play, 99
Practice session, planning, 12
Pride, 5
Punching the ball clear, 80–81
Punt, 77
Push up, 133

Quick turn, 38

Rebounds, 113
Receiving and turning on the ball, 44–46
Referees, 9
Reminiscence, 12
Responsibility, delegation of, 9
Rhythm, 17

Safety hints, 9
Safety rules, enforcement of, 7
Set pieces, 90, 133
Shielding, 46, 133
Shielding turn, 45
Shinguards, 9
Shinpads, 9
Shooting
drills in, 60–63
far-post shot, 62–63
improvised, 63–64
techniques, 59–61
Short corner, 94
Shot stopping, 73–75
Shots, narrowing angle of, 79–80
Sidefoot pass, 23
Sidelining the attacker, 133
Sideways dive, 73
Six-a-side soccer, 13–14, 115–16
Skill progressions, 133
Sliding tackle, 84, 133
Small-sided drill, 133

Soccer
    appeal of, 5
    basic laws of, 122
Soccer ball
    bringing down on the laces, 32–34
    distributing, 76–77
    jumping to head, 52–55
    number of, at practice, 6
    punching, clear, 80–81
    receiving and turning on, 44–46
    shielding, 46
    strengthening exercises with, 20
    stretching exercises with, 19
Soccer baseball, 113
Soccer golf, 113
Soccer play activities, 112–13
    "headers and volleys," 112
    rebounds, 113
    soccer baseball, 113
    soccer golf, 113
    soccer tennis, 113
    "29s," 112
    "3 and In," 112
Soccer skills awards, 120
Soccer tennis, 113
Socks, 9
Sportsmanship, 5
Strengthening exercises, 20
Stretching exercises, 19–20
Sweeper, 117, 133
Sweeper system, 117

Tackle, 133
Tackling, 84–85
Take on, 133
Target man, 133
Teaching
    ball juggling, 17–19
    versus coaching, 5
    grid system of, 10–12
    heading, 49–51
    hints in, 5–7

Team cooperation, 5
Team defense, 85–86
Team formations, 114
    eleven-a-side soccer, 13, 116–19
    six-a-side soccer, 13–14, 115–16
Team spirit, 5
Thigh, 16
Thigh control, 18, 32
Thigh juggling, 16, 18
3 and In, 112
Throw-head-catch, 111
Throw-ins, 90
    tactics at, 91–92
Tie-up, 133
29s, 112
Two-fisted punch, 80
Two-handed catch, 80
2-1-2 formation, 115
2-2-1 formation, 115, 116

Underhand roll, 76
Unopposed soccer, 112

Volley, 64, 133
    drills for, 66
    types of kicks, 65
Volleying, for goal, 66–68

Wall pass, 103, 133
Warming up, 12, 21
    calisthenics, 21
    juggling, 16–19
    strengthening exercises, 20
    stretching exercises, 19–20
Water breaks, 7
Whistle, correct use of, 7
Winger plays, 118
Winning, concept of, 5

Zone defense, 133
Zone marking system, 116